W9-BUT-295

Manuals, 12

The Sheffield Manual
for Authors and Editors
in Biblical Studies

The
SHEFFIELD MANUAL

for AUTHORS & EDITORS
in BIBLICAL STUDIES

David J.A. Clines

Sheffield
Academic Press

Published by Sheffield Academic Press Ltd
Mansion House
19 Kingfield Road
Sheffield S11 9AS
England

Printed on acid-free paper in Great Britain
The Cromwell Press
Melksham, Wiltshire

British Library Cataloguing in Publication Data

A catalogue record for this book is available
from the British Library

ISBN 1-85075-727-5

CONTENTS

96738

C. REFERENCE

PREFACE

The origins of this Housestyle Manual are beyond recall. Since the beginnings of Sheffield Academic Press go back twenty years now, no one can remember how the first decisions were made about how our books and journals should look, and what rules should govern the text of articles and books we publish.

To tell the truth, when we began to publish journals and books, we took the rather idealistic view that authors should be free to use whatever editing conventions they chose, and that publishers should not interfere with the way academic authors chose to present their work. But we soon came to realize that even academic authors cannot always be relied on to produce a technically perfect manuscript, and that the best of us can deliver manuscripts with many minor inconsistencies, misspellings, grammatical errors, verbal infelicities and the like. To decipher each author's system of writing bibliographic references in footnotes, for example, and then to ensure that the same system is used consistently throughout the article or the book is, we discovered, more troublesome than to develop a single system or housestyle and to apply that to every publication.

So, learning from experience, and this we do remember, for quite a few years there has been in existence some version or another of this Housestyle Manual, and successive editors at the Press have contributed to the elaboration of it. I myself know that in 1992 I prepared an 86-page version of the Manual, which has been in use since that time by SAP's editors and by academic editors publishing with the Press. Though it was elaborate, that Manual was by no means comprehensive, and it has become increasingly obvious that a more systematic and tightly edited manual was needed both by the Press's editors and by editors of journals, and of collected volumes and the like. So, with the help of the current desk editors at SAP, I have prepared this revision.

There are several different groups I have had in mind when

composing this Manual (their identities are further revealed in the Introduction), and I have tried as far as possible to distinguish what I imagine their needs to be. Many sets of needs overlap—for example, both authors and copy-editors need to have ready to hand extensive lists of abbreviations of the names of biblical books and of scholarly journals. It made sense therefore to combine the various kinds of material in one publication; but inevitably there will be not a little that is irrelevant to one kind of user or another, and I crave the indulgence of readers if some material is superfluous to their own needs.

This is a book of rules; and yet it has no authority, except for those employed by the Press to execute those rules. For authors who are publishing with SAP, it is an encouragement to conform their manuscript as far as possible to our housestyle, and a preview of the format in which their work will be edited. For others, it is nothing but the exemplification of a style, and they can take it or leave it as they see fit. Many of the rules in this Manual are fundamentally arbitrary, it must be said. It is an arbitrary matter, for example, whether one refers to a biblical text as Gen 12:1 or Gen xii 1 or Gn. 12.1 or Gen. 12,1 or any combination of these forms. On the other hand, there are rules in this Manual that concern issues of right and wrong, as absolute as any that may be encountered in a postmodern age. In spelling, for instance, though there are permitted variants, there is a definitive rightness; and although the rightness is no more than a social convention of our own days, none of us, author or editor or publisher, wants to offend against it. As with most matters that are dealt with in this Manual, the art in preparing a manuscript for publication is to conceal art: to create an unobserved smoothness and an invisible consistency that never draw attention to themselves.

A manual of this kind can never be made up from scratch, since the conventions of editing and publishing are rather conservative and traditional. No one wants to read a published book in which the editing standards are so novel and creative that they distract attention from the subject matter of the book itself. So this Manual too has antecedents. Its origins go back, in matters of editing, to Hart's *Rules for Compositors and*

Readers, in matters of English style to Fowler's *Modern English Usage*, and in matters of spelling to *The Concise Oxford Dictionary*. These days, there are other authorities too, whose advice has always to be taken into account: principal among them are the *Chicago Manual of Style*, the most compendious of all our reference works, and Butcher's *Copy-Editing*, a helpful work in the Cambridge tradition. For spelling, our default reference work is now *Collins Dictionary*, which we value for its inclusion of both British and American spellings, and for its notation of the correct places in which any given word should be hyphenated (regrettably omitted from the latest edition).

So much for the editorial tradition in which Sheffield Academic Press stands. Perhaps Sheffield seems a little old-fashioned, writing (in British spelling) *mediaeval* rather than *medieval* and insisting on 'pp.' and the like; but these are minor matters. What it really cares about is quality, and its editors know that, however difficult excellence and accuracy may be to achieve, there is only one standard at which authors and editors and publishers should aim: absolute perfection.

DJAC
31.12.96

ADDRESS LIST
FOR SHEFFIELD ACADEMIC PRESS

Street Address
Sheffield Academic Press, Mansion House, 19 Kingfield Road, Sheffield S11 9AS, England

Telephone
+44 (0)114 255 4433

Fax
+44 (0)114 255 4626

E-mail
admin@sheffac.demon.co.uk
(individual staff may be addressed in the form: JAllen@sheffac.demon.co.uk)

Web Site
http://www.shef-ac-press.co.uk

North American Address
Sheffield Academic Press, c/o Cornell University Press Services, PO Box 6525, Ithaca, NY 14851, USA

Correspondence about proposed manuscripts should be addressed to The Publishers (or to Professor David J.A. Clines or Professor Philip R. Davies individually [e-mail d.clines@ Sheffield.ac.uk and p.davies@Sheffield.ac.uk]).

Correspondence about business matters should be addressed to the Managing Director, Mrs Jean Allen.

A. Introductions

This Manual has been designed for several different groups of users:

- authors intending to submit a manuscript to Sheffield Academic Press (SAP) with a view to publication
- contracted authors who are revising their manuscripts in accordance with the housestyle of the Press
- academic editors of books and journals published by SAP
- editors of SAP journals and of books of essays, Festschriften and the like
- in-house desk editors and copy-editors, and freelance copy-editors, proofreaders and indexers
- authors needing advice on the preparation of their manuscript in biblical studies or related fields for submission to a publisher who does not make specific requirements for style.

1. THIS MANUAL

1.1 Some of the material here will be specific for SAP authors, and may be ignored by other readers. But there does seem to be a need for a Manual such as this within the community of biblical scholars generally. The guidelines of the Society of Biblical Literature are extremely helpful—and indeed the SAP style is intended to harmonize with them as much as possible. But there are many matters that an author needs to know that are not covered by the SBL rules, and, as far as we know, there is not another ready source of information tailored to the needs of biblical scholars. (For differences between SAP and SBL styles, see §32 below.)

1.2 This Manual has gone through several transformations in the course of the last few years at Sheffield Academic Press. In previous versions it has been constantly in the hands of in-house editors, series editors and editors of collective volumes, and many suggestions have been incorporated from various persons. David Orton, Stanley Porter and John Jarick, formerly Senior Academic Editors at SAP, have contributed extensively to the text of this handbook, and a number of desk editors, Alison Bogle, Steve Barganski, Eric Christianson, Andrew Kirk, Webb Mealy, Carol Smith and Helen Tookey, have offered numerous comments and suggestions for improvement.

1.3 It is now time, we believe, for our in-house manual to be totally reworked, and made available to a wider public than those who have been using it. No work of this kind will ever be comprehensive or definitive, and suggestions for its future improvement and expansion will always be welcome.

1.4 One of the envisaged functions of this Manual is to enable scholars to recognize, from its detail and from the complexity of the material it contains, that the process of publishing is not simply a commercial operation but also the enhancement of the scholarly accuracy and excellence of the author's work.

2. Sheffield Academic Press

2.1 Sheffield Academic Press (SAP) is a scholarly publisher, producing books and journals for the academic community. At present, it publishes books and journals in the humanities, journals in biomedicine, and reference, professional and technical books in the sciences.

2.2 SAP is a private company. It is not owned by the University of Sheffield, and it receives no institutional subsidies. It pays all its own costs from its sales. It exists to serve the academic community rather than to make profit; but it needs annual profits not only to remain viable but also to expand.

2.3 SAP is free from dominance by the market, by shareholders, by academic committees or by institutional inertia. It believes in publishing scholarly work of quality, to the highest standards. It invests in every book and every journal an unusually high level of editorial work so as to make all its publications as perfect as possible.

2.4 SAP has four Directors, one, the chairman of the board, an accountant and businessman (Michael J. Mallett), one, the managing director responsible for the day-to-day running of the company (Jean Allen), and two who are also the Press's Publishers in the humanities (David J.A. Clines and Philip R. Davies). (Graeme MacKintosh is the Press's Publisher in science.)

2.5 SAP is situated in a large Victorian stone-built house in a leafy suburb of Sheffield, the fifth largest city in England. It has cordial relations with Sheffield's two universities, the University of Sheffield and Sheffield Hallam University (which together have over 40,000 students), but it regards its remit as international. In fact about half its authors are from outside the United Kingdom, and more than half its books and journals are sold to customers abroad.

The History of the Press

2.6   The Press's history may be said to have begun in 1976 when three lecturers in the Department of Biblical Studies in the University of Sheffield (David Clines, Philip Davies and David Gunn) decided that it was time to launch a new journal, which they named *Journal for the Study of the Old Testament*. Its aims were, on the one hand, to enable rapid and informal publication, and on the other, to create a vehicle for newly developing approaches to the Old Testament which the traditional journals may have had difficulty in accepting.

2.7   Before long, a supplement series of monographs began to be published, and in 1979 a sister journal, *Journal for the Study of the New Testament*, was launched. By this time it was evident that the publishing project, which had lodged in the Department of Biblical Studies, needed an identity and home of its own, and it became JSOT Press.

2.8   The Press expanded, and with it the horizons of its Publishers, who determined that it should aim to become a general academic press, not devoted to biblical studies alone, as it had been, but open to development in any scholarly field. In the late 1980s, the name of the Press became Sheffield Academic Press, in order to reflect that wider orientation, though the copyright line for biblical books remained JSOT Press until 1994.

2.9   SAP then began to publish in archaeology, history, modern languages and literature. In the 1990s, it acquired a publishing concern known as SUBIS (Sheffield University Biomedical Service), which publishes about 100 fortnightly bibliographical bulletins, and in 1994 J.R. Collis Publications, an independent archaeological publisher, merged with SAP. In 1996 it initiated a new division of reference, technical and professional books in the sciences.

2.10   By the end of 1997, SAP (which is to say, Sheffield Academic Press including JSOT Press) will have published its 1000th title. Of those 1000, over 850 are books, all but 50 or so of them being still in print; there are as well 20 journals in addition to the 100 SUBIS Bulletins. Biblical studies remains the core of the SAP business, and SAP likes to believe (though it is difficult to be sure in such matters) that it publishes more academic books in biblical studies than anyone else in the world.

3. Making a Book

3.1   Contrary to common opinion, authors do not make books; they prepare typescripts. It is publishers who make books, and they do that by turning authors' typescripts into books. The relationship between authors and publishers is surprisingly poorly understood by authors whose careers, and even their livelihoods, depend upon the publishing of their books, and the processes by which a manuscript is turned into a book, though fascinating in themselves, are very often ignored by authors.

3.1.1 In this section there will be detailed the stages by which a typescript (or, a manuscript, as it is still termed even though no publisher would consider a handwritten manuscript!) is turned into a book by Sheffield Academic Press; the processes will be similar, though not identical, for most scholarly publishers.

a. *Editorial Selection*

3.2   The first stage in the publication process is the evaluation and selection of manuscripts. SAP accepts for publication only those typescripts that have been approved by an academic editor or editorial board, who are appointed, but not employed, by the Press. Most manuscripts are submitted by authors to the editor(s) of the series they hope to be published in; and those manuscripts that are sent directly to the Press are delivered immediately to the appropriate academic editor(s).

3.3   The series editors recommend to the Press that a particular manuscript be published, and the Press then offers publication. In principle, the Press could refuse to accept an editor's recommendation, but in practice it does not usually question editors' judgments, and then only if the book proposed presents serious technical or financial problems to the Press.

b. *The Production Process*

3.4 When a manuscript is received by the Press from the series editor as ready for publication, it may have to wait some months before it can go into production, depending on the rate at which accepted manuscripts have been arriving. Once it has gone into production, it will normally be published within six to eight months.

3.5 The manuscript is assessed by the Managing Editor for the degree of its conformity to SAP housestyle. If the manuscript does not approximate to SAP housestyle, the author may be asked to revise the text accordingly.

3.6 When a manuscript has reached its turn to go into production, it is assigned to a desk editor at the Press. That editor is responsible for seeing the manuscript through all the stages of its production, and for liaising with the author. At an early stage the desk editor gets in touch with the author regarding the following matters: the planned schedule for the book, the author's likely availability for proofreading and indexing at the appropriate dates; information about the author and the book, for the purpose of publicity; establishing a list of journals to which the book will be sent for review.

3.7 The desk editor turns over the manuscript to a copy-editor (for the difference between the two roles, see §8.1), or perhaps undertakes the copy-editing role personally. The copy-editor's primary duty is to read the manuscript with the utmost care, checking spelling, punctuation, grammar, references, adherence to the housestyle of the Press, and consistency in general. (It may be noted that several of the major scholarly publishers dispense with a copy-editing of manuscripts; the technical quality of their books is inevitably inferior.) Sheffield rarely publishes a manuscript in the form in which it has been submitted by the author.

3.8 The desk editor works closely with the typesetter (who is usually employed in-house at the Press) to whom the book is assigned, so that together they know in detail the idiosyncrasies of the manuscript and can create a uniform and coherent style for it.

c. *The Stages of Production*

3.9 The early stages of production differ according to whether the manuscript has been received in hard copy only (i.e. as a typescript) or in a disk version.

3.10 In the case of manuscripts received in disk form, the first step is to convert the author's disk version into Microsoft Word 5 on the Press's Macintosh system. The typesetter at this stage makes a number of global checks and replacements (like inserting 'p.' and 'pp.' before page numbers if they are not present). See §37 for a checklist of these operations. The printout of the resulting text is known as Proof 1, and it is that text of the work that the copy-editor works on. The provision of an electronic version of the manuscript by the author does not bypass the copy-editing process, which has been found to be essential for the accuracy and consistency of the great majority of manuscripts.

3.11 In the case of manuscripts received in hard copy only, the author's typescript serves as Proof 1, and it is that typescript that the copy-editor marks up.

3.12 The copy-editor now proceeds to work through the manuscript. The stages of that task are outlined in §8.

3.13 While the manuscript is undergoing the initial production stages at the Press, the author is requested to begin preparing the indexes. Further details on indexing may be found at §4.16 and §23.

3.14 When the copy-editor has finished work on the manuscript, the work is checked by the desk editor, and Proof 1 goes to the typesetter, who makes all the changes indicated. When those corrections have been made, a laser-printed proof of the pages (Proof 2) is given to the copy-editor, who checks that all the corrections marked on Proof 1 have in fact been made. The copy-editor marks on Proof 2 any further corrections that need to be made, and transfers from Proof 1 to Proof 2 any queries to the author that need to be answered.

3.15 Proof 2 is a page proof of the whole text of the book, together with title page, front matter (e.g. contents page, list of abbreviations), and with running heads and page numbers (though the page numbers are not definitive at this stage).

3.16 Proof 2, together with a copy of Proof 1 (either the original or disk-read version), is then sent to the author for proofreading. The author returns to the Press the corrected proof (Proof 2).

3.17 The desk editor then checks the author's corrections, to ensure that they follow the conventions used throughout the book, and that all the queries to the author have been answered. The typesetter makes the corrections, and produces Proof 3. The desk editor again checks that the corrections have been properly made. Except in the case of unusually difficult books, a second proof is not sent to the author.

3.18 Once the text of the book has reached a definitive stage, and no more corrections will be made that will affect the pagination, the index or indexes are prepared. In cases where the indexed items have already been embedded in the text, the indexing program is run and the desk editor and typesetter finalize the indexes in the correct format. In other cases, the book is given to an indexer to prepare the index at this stage.

d. *Printing the Book*

3.19 When the book has achieved its final form, the text is printed out on individual sheets of paper on a high-quality laser printer, at a size 40% larger than the final pages of the book. These pages ('camera-ready copy') are sent to the printer, who photographs them at a reduced size (thus achieving greater clarity in the type) and prints them by photolithography. In some cases, the book is sent to the printer on disk, or via an ISDN telephone line, and text is set directly to film.

3.20 SAP's books are always printed on acid-free paper, for greater longevity. The sections or quires of the book (each 32 or 16 pages) are sewn (or, in the case of paperbacks, glued in the 'burst bound' process). The printer usually takes three to five weeks to manufacture the printed and bound copies.

3.21 When the bound books are delivered to SAP, shrink-wrapped in packets of 20 or so to protect them against damp and dust, they are warehoused immediately. On the day after delivery, the book is 'published'. Copies are dispatched to customers who have a standing order for the series in which the book is published, to customers who have ordered the book prior to its publication, to review journals, and to the author. When the author lives abroad, one of the author's complimentary copies is sent by airmail.

e. *Publicizing the Book*

3.22 From the earliest stages in the book's production, the author's aid will have been enlisted in enabling SAP to market the book effectively. Suggestions from the author about review journals, scholarly conferences, possible textbook adoptions and the like are incorporated within SAP's own experience of selling academic books.

3.23 Every book published by SAP is listed in its twice-yearly catalogues. In a book's first year (when it is still 'Frontlist') it is naturally given more exposure than in later years, but, unlike many other publishers, SAP never stops publicizing its backlist titles. Its complete annual catalogues are arranged by topic, and each book still in print is listed in its appropriate place.

3.24 New books are advertised in the monthly flyers sent out in every packet of books dispatched by SAP.

3.25 SAP books are exhibited and sold at many scholarly conventions worldwide each year.

3.26 Information about all SAP books and journals is constantly accessible and regularly updated in the Press's Web site (http://www.shef-ac-press.co.uk). Customers can order directly from the Web site by e-mail.

3.27 SAP employs sales representatives throughout the world, who solicit orders from booksellers.

3.28 Review copies are freely sent to scholarly journals; authors are asked to suggest the names of review journals known to them in addition to those to which the Press sends review copies as a matter of course.

3.29 Orders are received by mail, e-mail, telephone, fax and (in the UK) from bookshops by Tele-ordering.

f. *Selling the Book*

3.30 The Press will have printed enough copies to keep the book in print for five years, and preferably for ten, judging by the sales of comparable titles. It is a matter of principle with the Press to endeavour to keep scholarly books in print as long as possible. Of the 1000 titles the Press has published, only about 50 have been allowed to go out of print (although some others may be temporarily out of print, for which the technical term is 'reprinting'). A reprint of a scholarly monograph is usually uneconomical, but a book in demand as a textbook may go through several printings (or editions, if the author makes substantial alterations for a new printing).

3.31 The Press sells its academic books mainly by direct mail, and publicizes its titles mainly to its own customers, since they are the institutions and individuals that are most likely to be interested in current titles.

3.32 The Press's sales pledge is to process an order the day it arrives, and to dispatch the books or journals ordered the following working day. Books ordered are sent directly from Sheffield; to overseas customers they are sent by air freight, so that customers in the USA, for example, may expect to receive their order in 7 to 21 days from the date of order.

3.33 Customers in North America may order from the Press's distributor in North America, Cornell University Press Services (see p. 10 for address and phone number).

3.34 SAP publishes two catalogues in Biblical Studies each year: in May a complete catalogue of all in-print titles, with announcements of autumn and winter books, and in November a catalogue of forthcoming spring and summer books. In both catalogues the titles are arranged by category so as to assist readers to locate all the titles in their specialist areas. In the complete catalogue all the Backlist titles are listed at the foot of the relevant category page.

4. THE ROLE OF THE AUTHOR

4.1 *How Do I Approach the Press with a Book Proposal?*
Whether the manuscript is complete, or whether you have just an outline, a proposal or some sample chapters, you should send your material to The Publishers, Sheffield Academic Press, Mansion House, 19 Kingfield Road, Sheffield S11 9AS, England. You can address it to one or both of the two Publishers in the humanities (Professor David J.A. Clines and Professor Philip R. Davies).

4.2 *What Kinds of Books Do you Consider?*
Only academic books. If your manuscript has no footnotes and bibliography, it is probably not an academic book. At present, we are accepting proposals only in the humanities. Although we publish in some areas of science, all our publications in those fields are commissioned by us, and we do not consider unsolicited manuscripts.

4.3 *What Is your Review Process?*
All book proposals received are either passed to the editor or executive editor of one of our series, or, if there is no appropriate series, considered by the Publishers themselves. In the case of a series book, the editor asks a member or members of the editorial board for their evaluation. In the light of their reports, a decision is made and is communicated to you and to the Press. The series editors recommend to the Press that a particular manuscript be published, and the Press then offers a contract of publication. In principle, the Press could refuse to accept an editor's recommendation, but in practice it does not question editors' judgments, unless the proposed book raises severe technical or financial problems that need to be negotiated.

4.4 *How Long Does the Review Process Take?*
The academic editor or editorial board are appointed, but not

employed, by the Press. The Press records the progress of manu-scripts that are undergoing editorial evaluation, but in general it awaits the series editor's decision. Such editors are carrying out their role as part of their academic duties, and they are not paid by the Press to do so; the Press therefore cannot insist that they prioritize their editorial work.

4.4.1 Please allow three months after submission of your manu-script or proposal before enquiring about the progress of the review. A longer or shorter time taken by the process does not imply anything about the likely outcome; it is simply a function of the availability of the reader of your manuscript!

4.5 *Will I Be Asked to Revise the Manuscript?*
Perhaps so. If there are substantial revisions to be made before the manuscript is acceptable, the series editor will confirm that you are willing to make them before SAP offers you a contract. The series editor may say, for example, that Chapter 1 should be eliminated, and Chapter 3 should be greatly reduced in size, or some such thing. If you have been asked to make such sub-stantive revisions, you should return your revised manuscript to the series editor for approval once you have completed the work.

4.5.1 It may be that the series editor asks you to revise your manuscript for more technical reasons, for example to reduce the amount of Hebrew type or to bring the format of footnotes more into line with SAP housestyle. In such cases, you should not return your revised manuscript to the series editor, but directly to the Press (addressed to the Managing Editor).

4.6 *How Is Having a Book Commissioned Different?*
So far this chapter has been about those books that have been 'proposed', that is, submitted to the Press by an author. SAP, however, also publishes 'commissioned' books. Commissioned manuscripts may have been suggested by a series editor, an editor at the Press, or, indeed, by their author; but however the idea of the manuscript has arisen, such manuscripts differ from 'proposed' manuscripts in that they have been contracted for

before they are written (or, finished). The Press is obliged to accept manuscripts it has commissioned—except in the unlikely event of the completed manuscript not fulfilling the agreed intentions for the work or being below a reasonable standard.

4.7   *If my Book Is Accepted, Do I Get a Contract?*
Yes, if your manuscript (or proposal) is accepted by the series editor or Publishers, you will be offered a contract of publication by the Press. If the book is not completed or if the manuscript needs revision, a date by which the manuscript is expected is written into the contract. No penalty attaches to late submission of a manuscript, but the Press encourages authors whose manuscripts are overdue to let the Press know the likely date of submission. The Press is not bound by a contract of publication to publish a book that has arrived later than the contracted date; but in practice, since the Press exists to publish books, it is always happy to receive a manuscript.

4.7.1 The normal terms of contract offered by the Press are these: publication at the Press's expense without subvention (though this term may be varied in the case of unusually expensive or difficult books, or books for which an exceptionally small sale is expected); six complimentary copies of the published book for the author; in the case of an 'established' author (which SAP defines as someone who has previously published a scholarly book, not necessarily with SAP), a royalty of ten percent of net receipts (which amounts to about six percent of the gross receipts from sales of the book).

4.8   *What about Permissions?*
Acquiring permission for lengthy quotations from other works or for graphic images is the responsibility of the author, who is also responsible for payment of any fees for permissions (authors who are to receive royalties may ask the Press to pay such fees as a charge against their royalties). See further, §10.5.

4.9   *How Important Is the Title?*
Very. It does not matter much if the title of the manuscript submitted is wordy or lacking in punch. No manuscript was ever

turned down because its working title was not very attractive. Like all publishers, SAP expects to work with its authors on shaping the most appealing and most appropriate title for each of its books. Among words less likely to be favoured for a title are 'studies', 'new', 'essays', foreign words, highly allusive phrases, words in inverted commas. Authors may find it helpful when devising a title to study the titles of books SAP has already published. In our opinion, some of our more successful recent titles are these:

> *Striking New Images: Roman Imperial Coinage and the New Testament World*
>
> *Plotted, Shot, and Painted: Cultural Representations of Biblical Women*
>
> *By Philosophy and Empty Deceit: Colossians as Response to a Cynic Critique*
>
> *Liberating Paul: The Justice of God and the Politics of the Apostle*
>
> *Chained in Christ: The Experience and Rhetoric of Paul's Imprisonments*
>
> *Spikenard and Saffron: The Imagery of the Song of Songs.*

4.10 *Who Decides on the Title?*
As with most publishers, SAP's contracts specify that the publishers are ultimately responsible for the title of a book. But it is equally SAP's policy to work closely with the author on the title of their book, and authors may be reassured to know that the Press gives the highest regard to the wishes of authors in this important matter.

4.11 *Should I Present my Manuscript on Disk?*
When you are submitting your manuscript for evaluation, only a hard copy version should be sent, but it is helpful to know at the time of submission whether a disk version could be made available to the Press, and if so, in what format.

4.11.1 If your manuscript is accepted, we would appreciate having it on disk, especially if you use one of the most common word processors, like Microsoft Word or Word for Windows or Windows 95 or WordPerfect. With other wordprocessing software, it is best to check with the Press before going to any trouble to prepare disks. Many authors, however, simply send copies of their own disks as a matter of course, and this is quite acceptable. Authors should, however, be aware that the Press cannot guarantee to publish manuscripts from the disk version.

4.12 *Do you Want a Hard Copy as Well?*
Yes, please. It should correspond exactly with the disk version. It should be printed double-spaced, and the footnotes also (preferably at the foot of the page they refer to) should be double-spaced.

4.13 *Do you Want Camera-Ready Copy?*
Not normally, but if you are very interested in typography and would like to imitate the Press's style of point sizes, line-spacing, margins, etc., the parameters the Press uses will be found in Section C of this Manual.

4.14 *What If I am Sending Only a Typescript, without a Disk?*
Please print your text double-spaced, and the footnotes (preferably at the foot of the page they refer to) should also be double-spaced if possible. Pages should always be numbered sequentially throughout the whole manuscript, and there should be a table of contents with the page numbers for each chapter.

4.15 *What Special Rules Should I Observe?*
The same advice applies to all authors, whether they are planning to submit their work on disk or as typescript. Absolute accuracy and absolute consistency must be the standard for scholarly publishing; this Manual will serve as a guide to the kinds of detail that authors should be paying attention to. There follow some notes on particular aspects of a manuscript that need special care.

4.15.1 *Spelling.* If you are preparing your work on a word-processor, be sure to use its spellchecker—and at the very last stage (more errors occur in the last-minute revisions than at any other stage of preparation of the manuscript). If you are typing your manuscript, all authors except the very best spellers should ask someone else to read the entire manuscript for surface errors like those in spelling.

4.15.2 *Accents* on Greek, transliteration of Hebrew, copying of quotations in German, French, etc. Our experience is that not more than one in fifty manuscripts will have five lines of Greek or transliterated Hebrew free of error (commonly the maqqeph is not represented by a hyphen, or a long vowel does not have a macron above it). Not more than one in ten manuscripts, we find, quote German or Hebrew for five lines without a mistake. Please check and double-check your foreign language materials, since it may well be that you are the only expert in those languages who will see your manuscript in the course of its production.

4.15.3 *Biblical book abbreviations.* Please note the system used by the Press. It is somewhat different from the SBL system (see §4.15.9). Please understand from this Manual the places where the name of a biblical book should be written in full, and the places where it should be abbreviated.

4.15.4 *Position of closing quotation marks.* It is a somewhat arbitrary decision whether a punctuation mark should be inside or outside a closing quotation mark, but it is essential that some norm should be adopted and adhered to. The Press follows one of the established British systems, set out in detail in §18. Any author who takes the trouble to carry out the Press's system has found the way to our heart.

4.15.5 *Bibliographical references in footnotes.* Again, while there is no absolutely right way for referring to books and articles, the Press has adopted a system that it believes is logical, and it requests authors to adhere to it rigidly. If different books published by the Press use different systems, there is a high chance of inconsistency within a single work creeping in.

4.15.6 *Consistency* in the appearance, use and numbering of headings throughout chapters. Headings are important navigational aids to the reader, and everything possible should be done to make them plain and logical, as well as consistent.

4.15.7 *Diagrams, plates, tables, maps, etc.* Proper labelling of matter extraneous to the text itself is absolutely indispensable. It is also important to indicate the point in the text to which the nontextual matter refers, and to note how near to or far from the text itself the typesetter can insert it.

4.15.8 *Internal cross-references* to pages in the manuscript should be totally eliminated—as far as is humanly possible. Occasionally a work needs references in the footnotes to other footnotes; this is acceptable. When other cross-references are needed, they should be made to chapters and numbered sections in chapters. It is a nightmare for the copy-editor when there are cross-references to pages in a book, since the exact pagination of any work is in constant flux until the last moment in the type-setting process, and it is sometimes a major undertaking to discover the point in the manuscript to which the cross-reference is meant to refer.

4.15.9 If you are used to preparing manuscripts in the Society of Biblical Literature (SBL) format, you will find that SAP's housestyle is very similar. There is a checklist in Section C of this Manual (§32) of the points at which the SAP style differs from that of SBL.

4.16 *What about Indexes?*
The first thing is to establish what indexes are appropriate. In our monographs on biblical subjects, we usually have only an index of biblical passages (and perhaps of other ancient sources) referred to and of authors cited. A subject index is usually not necessary in a monograph, but in a textbook or collection of essays it is more likely to be valuable.

4.16.1 The second issue is who is going to provide the indexes to your book. The indexing of your book is your responsibility. If you are unable to provide indexes (usually biblical reference and author indexes only), the Press will arrange to produce them, but at your cost. For a monograph of c. 225 pages, the indexes usually cost about £100, which can be charged against your royalties.

4.16.2 If you do provide indexes, there are two moments when you can do it. The first, and by far the better, is before you submit the final form of the manuscript or before the accepted manuscript goes into production. Especially if you are working in Microsoft Word, you can embed indexing tags in the text (in 'hidden text'). Then when the pagination of the book is finalized, the Press's typesetters can run the index program and include all the items you have specified. (For instructions on how to index a book in Microsoft Word, see Section C of this Manual, §35.) The great advantage of embedding index tags in the book is that when your book comes to be available on CD-ROM (as we expect all SAP books will be eventually), the CD's search engine will be able to locate the places where you have referred to a particular text or particular author.

4.16.3 The second point at which you can prepare an index is between the acceptance of your manuscript and receiving the page proofs. In this method, what you prepare is a list of the items that are to be indexed, in which the Press's indexer fills in the page numbers once the pagination is finalized.

4.16.4 If you are unable or unwilling to prepare the indexes yourself, the Press will employ someone either to embed indexing tags in your manuscript at the Proof 1 stage, or to index the book manually when the final pagination is known.

4.17 *What Advice Have you for How I Write my Manuscript?*
Works of research are not usually literary masterpieces, but idiomatic English is expected by readers. There should be an even flow in the writing, avoiding where possible over-long and over-short sentences, repetitiveness, redundancies, excessive use of the first person (especially plural), unnecessarily florid language, etc. Paragraphs should not normally extend over one full page of text (c. 400 words).

4.17.1 If English is not your native language, or if you feel inconfident about your written English, please let your desk editor know to what extent you would like him or her to intervene in the wording of your manuscript. Unless the desk editor hears otherwise from the author, the copy-editor is under instruction not to alter the wording of an author, except to correct obvious errors. All changes to an author's manuscript, whether proposed or provisionally made already, are in any case marked on Proof 1, a copy of which is sent to the author.

4.18 *Do I Get Proofs?*

Yes. After your book has been typeset by SAP, it is proofread for sense (not word for word against the original) by the Press, and only then is a proof sent to you. That proof may have some corrections already marked on it by the copy-editor, but the main responsibility for the proofreading is your own. You are advised in particular to check all numerals, cross-references and any foreign language material. And you are urged to find someone else in addition to yourself to proofread your work.

4.18.1 You should mark errors in the proofs in black or blue (not in red, which SAP uses for its in-house corrections). Please be aware that a large number of alterations to your text at this stage will incur a charge.

5. The Role of the Editor
of a Collected Volume

5.1   Scholars sometimes wish to propose a volume of collected essays, perhaps arising from a conference, or in honour of a distinguished scholar (e.g. a Festschrift).

5.2   The editor or editors of such a proposed volume should write to one of the Publishers at Sheffield Academic Press (Professor David J.A. Clines and Professor Philip R. Davies), outlining the contents of the proposed volume and the contributors envisaged. A decision will be made on the basis of the standing of the proposed contributors and (in the case of honorary volumes) of the scholar to whom it is being dedicated.

5.3   If the decision is positive, the Press enters into a contract with the editor or editors of the volume (not with the individual contributors). If there is a particular date by which the volume should ideally be published, it is helpful that this should be mentioned as soon as possible.

5.4   The editor(s) are responsible for selecting the contributors to the volume, for communicating to them the essentials of the Press's housestyle (a brief outline is made available to editors), and for receiving manuscripts from authors. The editor(s) should edit the contributions for sense and accuracy, referring them back to contributors when necessary, and seeking the approval of authors for any proposed changes of wording to the author's text.

5.5   The editor(s) guarantee to the Press the academic quality of the work.

5.6   Such a collective work undergoes the same copy-editing process at SAP as the work of an individual author. Proofs are sent both to the authors of the contributions and to the editor(s). Contributors return their proofs to the editor(s), who combine the author's and the editor's corrections on a single proof, which the editor(s) then return to the Press.

5.7 Each editor is entitled to receive two complimentary copies of the work, and each author receives one copy of the work in lieu of offprints.

6. THE ROLE OF THE EDITOR OF A JOURNAL

6.1   The editor of a journal published by SAP is appointed by the Publishers of the Press. There is an editorial board associated with each journal. It is usually the editor who makes nominations for the appointment or the termination of appointment of members of the editorial board, and the Publishers on behalf of the Press extend invitations (or thanks for services rendered) in the light of the editor's suggestions.

6.2   The role of the journal editor is in the first place to select articles from among those sent by authors for publication. In making a selection, the editor has recourse to the members of the editorial board, evaluating the reports from them as readers. The editor is aware of the number of articles that can be published in the journal each year, and monitors the effect of acceptances on any backlog that is created.

6.3   The role of the journal editor is in the second place to encourage authors to submit suitable manuscripts for the journal. Whether or not an article is solicited by the editor or a member of the editorial board, it remains subject to the same editorial refereeing process as an article submitted spontaneously by its author.

6.4   Some journal editors prefer to work with a system of 'blind reviewing', in which the readers of manuscripts are not informed of the name of the authors. The Press takes no view on this matter, which it regards as one of editorial policy rather than of the Press's policy.

6.5   The journal editor is aware of the importance to authors of timely decisions, and is expected to reach a decision about a given manuscript within three months wherever possible, and in any case within six months.

6.6   The journal editor guarantees to the Press the academic quality of the articles accepted for the journal. If the journal editor requires substantive revision to a manuscript before he or she accepts it for publication, the manuscript is returned to the author and the revised manuscript must be approved by the journal editor before it is put into production by the Press.

7. The Role of the Editor of a Series

7.1 The editor of a series of books published by SAP is appointed by the Publishers of the Press. Usually there is an editorial board associated with each series. The editor makes nominations for the appointment or the termination of appointment of members of the editorial board, and the Publishers on behalf of the Press extend invitations (or thanks for services rendered) in the light of the editor's suggestions.

7.2 The role of the series editor is in the first place to select books from among those proposed by authors to the Press. In making a selection, the editor has recourse to the members of the editorial board, evaluating the reports from them as readers. Each series has a nominal quota of titles to be published each year, and the Press cannot undertake to publish more than the agreed total for the year.

7.3 The role of the series editor is in the second place to encourage authors to submit suitable manuscripts for the series. If the series editor knows of a work in progress by an established scholar that should be commissioned (i.e. contracted for, even before it is completed), the series editor should communicate with the Publishers of the Press.

7.4 The series editor is aware of the importance to authors of timely decisions, and is expected to reach a decision about a given manuscript within three months wherever possible, and in any case within six months.

7.5 The series editor either rejects a manuscript on behalf of the Press, or alternatively recommends publication of a manuscript to the Press. The Press does not undertake to issue a contract to any author or to publish any work even though recommended by the series editor. But in practice it is almost unknown for the recommendation of a series editor not to be accepted.

7.6   The series editor guarantees to the Press the academic quality of the work. If the series editor requires substantive revision to a manuscript before he or she recommends it for publication, the manuscript is returned to the author and the revised manuscript must be approved by the series editor before it is accepted by the Press.

7.7   The series editor and the editorial board receive complimentary copies of all the books published in the series during their period of office.

8. THE ROLE OF THE DESK EDITOR AND COPY-EDITOR

8.1   The terms 'desk editor' and 'copy-editor' are more or less interchangeable in publishing generally, but Sheffield Academic Press has found it useful to develop its own meanings for the terms. The Press employs several desk editors, who work full time at the Press's offices and whose duties are to supervise the passage of each title through the various stages from manuscript to finished book (a task that used to be called 'seeing a book through the press'). These desk editors copy-edit a number of titles themselves, but they also manage several freelance copy-editors, whose task is solely to prepare a manuscript for typesetting and to read the proofs. It is the desk editors who are the Press's principal contacts with authors, whether or not they are copy-editing their manuscripts personally.

8.2   The role of the copy-editor is in general to ensure that books and journals published by the Press conform to the Press's standards. In what follows in this chapter, the general procedures that copy-editors should follow are laid out. Thereafter in Section B of this handbook the detailed housestyle of Sheffield Academic Press, to which copy-editors should conform manuscripts, is spelled out, and, in Section C, a set of reference lists to which the copy-editor will have recourse during the work of copy-editing is provided.

8.3   Before a manuscript comes into the hands of the desk editor who will be responsible for it, it has completed all the necessary stages of approval by its academic editors. Their task will have been to certify to the Press the academic merit of the manuscript, and to assure the Press that detailed editorial work on it may now begin. Some academic editors will have made annotations on the manuscript, correcting errors, suggesting improvements in the English and so on; but others will have simply indicated that they have approved the manuscript for publication in the series they edit.

8.4   Before the copy-editing process proper begins, each manuscript is assessed by the Managing Editor in order to determine whether it is in fact ready to begin the process (for example, to check whether the author has carried out stylistic revisions already requested), or whether, even at this stage, it may be necessary to refer the manuscript back to the author for revision (for example, to conform the manuscript more closely to SAP housestyle). The Managing Editor also checks whether the manuscript poses any unusual problems from a production point of view (for example, does it contain a large number of illustrations, are there any special acknowledgments or copyright notices that must be included?), and then determines the scheduled month of publication.

8.5   Thereafter, the desk editor plans the detailed schedule for the book's production. The desk editor then writes to the author in order to introduce himself or herself, to check that the proposed production schedule will allow the author enough time to read proofs, to ask the author for any suggestions about the cover design (if the book is to have a specially designed cover or dustjacket) and to convey any suggested amendments to the title proposed by the Publishers. At the same time, the Author's Questionnaire is sent out, eliciting information that will be useful in publicizing and selling the book.

8.6   The desk editor then prepares a book checklist, which will accompany the manuscript through all the stages of its production. This Checklist, which will be added to in the course of the copy-editing, contains all notations peculiar to the specific book (for example, conventions about capitalizations or formats special to the book; is it using British or American spelling?). Once that Checklist is prepared, the mansucript is ready for the copy-editor, who may, as has been said above, be employed by the Press on a freelance basis.

8.7   If the manuscript has been received on disk, the typesetter carries out a number of routine revisions that may be necessary to bring the manuscript more into accord with SAP housestyle (e.g. replacing straight quotation marks with round or 'smart' quotes, inserting 'pp.' before page numbers). A checklist of the typesetter's alterations at this stage, known as disk cleanup, is provided in Section C of this Manual (§37). The printout of this version of the manuscript is called Proof 1, and it is this text that the copy-editor reads in detail and marks up.

8.8   The desk-editor begins the editing work on a book by getting to know the background to the manuscript. The desk-editor reviews the Correspondence File, which includes any correspondence between author and editors (series and desk editors), the Author's Questionnaire, a long and a short blurb about the book by the author, the Title Information sheet (from SAP's database, showing exact names of author(s), book, series, etc.), and a list of review journals to send the book to when it is published.

8.9   The next task of the desk-editor is to get to know the book as a whole. The desk-editor notes on the book checklist whether the complete manuscript is in hand, including the front matter, the text, the back matter, and any illustrations; sees how the chapters are structured, and whether this structure matches the table of contents; identifies whether bibliographic data are missing.

8.10   If the manuscript requires any art work, whether for the cover or for the book itself, or if it is intended that the book's typography should differ from SAP's usual styles, a design meeting is arranged by the desk editor. Those present include the Managing Director, the Graphic Designer and others relevant to the project. The Managing Director will ensure that the proposed art work or typography is referred to the Publishers for their approval.

8.11   The manuscript is now ready to be passed from the desk editor to the copy-editor along with the the book checklist and briefing letter. If the manuscript has been received in hard copy only, the copy-editor marks up the typsecript, and passes it to the typesetter for retyping ('inputting'). The printout of that text is also known as Proof 1. In such a case, the copy-editor will proofread Proof 1 for sense (that is, not word for word against the original manuscript) and to check that all the copy-editing alterations have been properly inserted in the text.

8.12 The copy-editing process proper starts with the Bibliography. This is likely to have inconsistencies and gaps; for example, the names of publishers may sometimes be missing (or lacking altogether), and the author may not have been aware of SAP's practice of citing in the Bibliography the full page references of articles (even if only a page is referred to in a footnote). The copy-editor or desk editor secures the missing information from the author (preferably in advance of the queries on the manuscript itself, since the bibliographical queries often take some time for the author to answer). In working with the Bibliography the copy-editor will become familiar, to some extent, with the works cited in the footnotes, and will be checking the form of citations for consistency against the Bibliography. The copy-editor notes on a copy of the Bibliography the short form of a book or article title employed by the author. By referring to that list in the course of copy-editing, the copy-editor will be able to detect cases where authors have mistakenly cited the short form of a work's title before they have given the full form, where they have incorrectly repeated the full form when they should have used the short form, and where they have inconsistently used more than one form of a short title. (Note that some authors give full bibliographical details on the first occasion a work is cited in a *chapter*, and this is acceptable.)

8.13 As the copy-editor works through the text, he or she notes on the Book Checklist any minor stylistic decisions made for the sake of consistency (such as capitalizations, italicizations, abbreviations, etc.), with a page reference to the first occurrence so that anyone can go back to it if necessary, and a little horizontal line to the left of the line of text in which it appears so that it can be found again easily.

8.14 The copy-editor uses blue or dark green ink for copy-editing on the author's typescript, or red ink on Proof 1 in the case of a book that has been read from a disk supplied by the author. If editing on the author's typescript, the copy-editor marks the text itself, except where it would be clearer to mark only the position of the correction in the text and to write the correction in full in the margin. If editing on Proof 1, the copy-editor makes all corrections in the margin with the appropriate mark in the text to indicate the position of the correction. The copy-editor will be aware that he or she is marking up the typescript or proof for the typesetter, and any marks that make the typesetter's work easier and more accurate are desirable.

8.15 The copy-editor uses capitals and lower-case letters in the appropriate form, being careful to form letters and punctuation as legibly as possible.

8.16 The proofreading marks used, following SAP's conventions, are shown in the table in Section C of this Manual (§36). Instructions to the typesetter are ringed by a circle or an oval; queries to the author are enclosed in a square or a rectangular box. The typesetter will understand that only letters and words not circled or boxed should be entered into the text. All instructions should clearly indicate the type of correction to be made and the location of the correction. For example, italics should be indicated by underlining the words to be italicized (unless of course they are already underlined or italicized in the manuscript).

8.17 When the copy-editor has finished work on Proof 1, the proof is given to the typesetter, either—in the case of a typescript that has arrived without a disk—for keyboarding ('inputting'), or—in the case of a manuscript that has come on disk—for corrections.

8.18 Once the corrections have been completed, the typesetter prints out Proof 2, and gives Proofs 1 and 2 to the copy-editor. The copy-editor then checks that all corrections have been done by the typesetter, marks on Proof 2 any that have not been done, and transfers to Proof 2 the square or rectangular boxes from Proof 1, which contain queries to the author.

8.19 It is important for authors and editors alike to know that everything produced by SAP is proofread in-house after it has been input or disk read (Proof 1). In this proofreading, the proofreader (who is usually the copy-editor) does not read word for word against copy (unless special circumstances such as the difficulty of the manuscript warrant it), but for any errors that may be noticed. The manuscript is kept to hand for consultation, and the proofreader glances at it frequently to check that the keyboarding or disk cleanup has been accurate and that major omissions of text, for example, have not occurred. During proofreading, everything about the manuscript is checked, including (but certainly not only) chapter headings, running heads and layouts, and the proof is read from beginning to end for typographical errors (literals), any remaining inconsistencies in the main text and footnotes, errors in punctuation, accidentally deleted text, etc. Other matters the copy-editor will be especially vigilant about will be: opening and closing quotation marks (especially the position of closing quotation marks relative to closing punctuation), opening and closing brackets (parentheses), British versus American spelling, consistency in the use of abbreviations and what they represent, footnote style with appropriate punctuation, internal cross-references (especially if page numbers are used), foreign languages, etc.

8.20 The Contents page is checked against the chapter headings to ensure that there is conformity word for word and in style. The page numbers are entered on the Contents page at each proof stage, even though they will probably be only provisional. Running heads are checked for each chapter. If the left- and right-hand running heads are correct on the first pages of a chapter, they can be assumed to be correct throughout that chapter (though not if, exceptionally, the chapter contains more than one 'section', in the terminology of Micrososft Word).

8.21 When the proofreader has completed reading a proof, the proofreader's initials and the date are written on the front cover of that proof. Every proof is numbered (Proof 1, etc.), as well as having a cover, so that the manuscript's production history can be tracked by the annotations on the proof itself. This notation is in addition to the Book Checklist.

8.22 The copy-editor then returns the manuscript (if any) and the proofs to the desk editor, who sends to the author a copy of both Proof 1 and the marked-up Proof 2, along with Notes to Authors on Proofs and details of the proofreading marks they should use. The author is asked to confirm receipt of proofs by phone, fax or e-mail. The author is asked to read the entire manuscript for sense, and to check that none of the corrections made to the original manuscript has wrongly altered the sense. The author is advised to find someone else as well to read the proofs, since authors are notoriously their own worst proof-readers (for example, it tends to be another person who notices when 'not' is missing or when the author has written 'more' when he or she means 'less').

8.23 The author returns to SAP only Proof 2. The desk editor or copy-editor checks the author's corrections to see that alterations and corrections conform to the housestyle and to the style for this book and that all the queries to the author have been answered satisfactorily. If there are many author's alterations, the desk editor arranges for the author to be charged for the cost of the newly introduced material.

8.24 Proof 2 next goes to the typesetter for the corrections to be implemented. When the typesetter has finished the corrections, he or she hyphenates the text and footnotes (according to the rules set out in the chapter on Hyphens and Dashes, in Section B of this Manual, §19.8). Proof 3 is then printed out, and returned to the desk editor or copy-editor to be checked against Proof 2 in order to ensure that all the corrections have been properly carried out.

8.25 Provided that no more corrections need to be made that will affect the pagination, the indexing of the book is now carried out. If indexing tags were inserted in the book at an earlier stage, the typesetter runs the indexing program, and works with the desk editor on formatting the results. If the book has not been preindexed in this way, the book is given to a freelance indexer, who prepares the index(es), whether on disk or as hard copy, which are then input if necessary and formatted by the typesetter. The desk editor then reads the index for consistency (though not word for word against the original).

8.26 Once the desk editor has approved the whole text of the book plus its indexes, the typesetter prints camera-ready copy (CRC) on high-quality paper (or prepares a disk to send to the printer, or a file to send to the printer electronically via an ISDN line). If the book is appearing in a series, and if there are available blank pages at the end of the book, the typesetter prepares for the end matter a list of books previously published in the series (by acquiring from the SAP database an up-to-date list and adding from that the titles that have been added since the last end-matter list was prepared). Such a list includes only books that have actually appeared or else are at the printers. They are listed in the order of their numbers in the series (not their date of publication), and, if there is not enough space to print the entire list, it is the more recent volumes that are listed. All books that have appeared in the series are listed; those that are out of print are so marked.

8.27 The desk editor finally checks, against the items called Finals on the Book Checklist, that all the parts of the book are complete: prelims (front matter), main text, indexes, end matter, cover, dustjacket (if any). The typesetter prepares a Print Order, which the desk editor checks and signs. The Managing Editor also checks the Print Order and the CRC and passes it to the Managing Director for approval before the book is sent to the printer.

B. Housestyle

In this Section there are set out the conventions or housestyle adopted by Sheffield for its books. Many of them are common to book publishers everywhere, others are more typical of British publishers in particular, and others are specific to Sheffield Academic Press.

The Press has found that a higher level of accuracy and efficiency is attained if a comprehensive housestyle is applied to all its publications. Deviation from the housestyle is permitted only in the case of unusual manuscripts and it must in each case be approved by the Publishers.

9. THE STRUCTURE OF A BOOK

9.1   *Front matter* consists of the following elements:

series title page
list of works by the same author
title page
bibliographical page
Dedication (may be on bibliographical page)
Table of Contents
tables of plates, maps, illustrations
Foreword
Preface
Acknowledgments
Abbreviations
List of Contributors
Introduction

9.2   Not all of these elements may be needed in any particular book, but, if they are, this is the order in which they should appear. A list of works by the same author appears on the first left-hand page, opposite the title page. Acknowledgments and Abbreviations can begin on a left-hand page provided that they do not directly follow the Contents page(s). If they do, they must start on a right-hand page. The series title page, title page, Contents, Foreword, Preface, List of Contributors and Introduction all begin on right-hand pages.

9.3   The *body* of the book is the text of the book proper. A book is almost invariably divided into chapters, chapters sometimes being grouped together in Parts. Parts are labelled 'Part A' or 'Part I' and so on; the name of the part has a page to itself (always a right-hand page, i.e. odd-numbered).

9.4   The first chapter in a book begins on a right-hand page, unless it follows a Part marker, in which case it begins on the next (left-hand) page. Following chapters begin on the next available page, even if that is a left-hand page. In some few cases, which will be annotated on the Book Checklist, there may be special reasons why chapters must always begin on a right-hand page (for example, if offprints of articles have been promised to the authors of a volume of collected essays). In some journals, articles always begin on a right-hand page (for the sake of offprints); in others, an article can begin on the first available page.

9.5 *Back matter* is arranged in the following order (not all elements may occur in any particular book, of course):

> Appendix(es)
> End-notes
> Bibliography
> Indexes.

Indexes are in the order:

> Biblical (and other ancient)
> Subjects
> Authors.

Appendixes, Notes, Bibliography and Indexes can start on a left- or right-hand page.

10. General Housestyle Rules

10.1 *Coding of Hebrew and Greek.* If the coding of Hebrew or Greek is required for the typesetter, the coding is to be written letter for letter left to right (i.e. with the code for each letter written directly above that letter, or in the same order in the margin). The coding for the Greek on the Macintosh is provided in Section C of this Manual, §29, below. The coding for Hebrew is provided in §30. Rules for the transliteration of Greek and Hebrew are found in the same place.

10.2 *Extent of Copy-Editor's Responsibility.* A copy-editor should correct any error found in a manuscript: misspelling, missed or misplaced accents, wrong Greek accents and breathings, inaccurate Hebrew vowel pointing, incorrect biblical references (if noticed), etc. If the copy-editor believes that the author has used the wrong word, or is mistaken or illogical or unclear, the copy-editor is at liberty to query the point politely with the author. In such cases the copy-editor writes a query in a square or rectangular box in the margin of the proof that will be sent to the author.

10.3 *Foreign scripts.* If there are foreign scripts in the manuscript, the copy-editor should check with the Publishers whether they should be typeset as they stand or should be transliterated or otherwise modified (e.g. by removing the vocalization of Hebrew). Any transliteration of Greek or Hebrew used should conform to the housestyle (see Section C of this Manual, §§29, 30). When authors have cited sentences in a foreign language (e.g. German, French) in the text of their work, they should be asked to provide a translation to be included in its place; in exceptional cases the original can also be given in a footnote. There is no need for authors to translate quotations in footnotes. The purpose of this rule is to ensure that the author's argument can be followed by readers who do not know the foreign language in question. And the rule does not apply to works about German or French literature, for example, where it may be assumed that the reader is familiar enough with the language not to require a translation.

10.4 *Gender-inclusive language.* SAP is committed to the use of gender-inclusive (non-sexist) language in all of its publications, and non-gender-inclusive language should be sensitively re-phrased; so copy-editors are under instruction to avoid 'he' when women also are intended, and to write 'humankind' or 'humanity' or 'humans' for 'mankind'. Plurals often solve the problem neatly (so 'readers find their interest aroused' for 'the reader finds his interest aroused'). Copy-editors should avoid 'he or she' whenever possible, and 's/he' at all costs. 'Their' is acceptable as a singular pronoun (e.g. 'No one in their right mind'). If the author will not accept such alterations, the Press will not insist, but will make clear nevertheless that such is its stated policy and that the use of inclusive language is not a matter of indifference to it.

10.5 *Permissions.* Acquiring permission for lengthy quotations from other works is the responsibility of individual authors (authors are also responsible for payment of any fees for permissions, but authors who are to receive royalties may ask the Press to pay such fees against their royalties). It is the desk editor's responsibility to ensure that these permissions are in hand. It is not necessary to pay a fee for use of up to 1000 words of the Revised Standard Version of the Bible (RSV), but the following wording is to be included on the bibliographic information page: 'The Scriptural quotations in this publication are from the Revised Standard Version of the Bible copyrighted 1971 and 1952 by the Division on Christian Education of the National Council of the Churches of Christ in the U.S.A.'

10.6 *Spelling.* Sheffield Academic Press, as an international publishing house, does not require authors to accommodate themselves to British style. In particular, American spellings and idioms are entirely acceptable, so long as the author is consistent. If an author wants to use American spelling, it does not matter that the author comes from some other part of the world than North America. There is no objection to American spelling even in book titles. But blurbs and other editorial matter emanating from SAP are always in British English. And SAP insists, even in books with American spelling, on British punctuation (for example, single quotation marks, punctuation usually outside quotation marks). Editors will not change acceptable American English expressions like 'in light of', 'likely' in the sense of 'probably', 'the seventh through the eighth century', or even 'different than' for 'different from' (though some American authors disapprove of the last of these idioms).

11. HEADINGS AND PAGE NUMBERS

11.1 The hierarchy and positioning of headings is a matter of much importance. In general a book is divided into chapters, which are numbered with Arabic numerals, 1, 2, etc. If the chapters are grouped in Parts, a separate right-hand page is given to the words Part I, Part II (or Part A, Part B), etc., with the title of that Part in upper case and small capitals, and the number of the Part in Roman numerals or capital letters. The next chapter usually follows on the immediately following page (but see also §9.4).

11.2 The title of a chapter is centred, on the fifth line of the page. The wording of the title is in small caps, using upper and lower case (upper case for the initial letter of the first word and of all words that are not prepositions, pronouns, articles or conjunctions, following the rules for capitalization in §16).

11.3 If the author's name follows a chapter title or article title (as in collected works and in journals), there is a blank line under the title, and the author's name is set in upper and lower case, centred. Between the title (or author's name, if it is given) and the beginning of the text, there are three blank lines.

11.4 There are several levels of heading. Text beginning under a heading is always ranged left, as is the opening paragraph of an article or chapter.

11.5 *The first level of heading* within a chapter will usually be centred, and may be numbered with an Arabic numeral in roman (not italic) type. The wording of the heading itself will usually be in upper and lower-case italics (upper case for the initial letter of the first word and all words that are not prepositions, pronouns, articles or conjunctions, following the rules for capitalization in §16). Upper and lower-case bold type is used for main headings in some series (especially OT Guides and NT Guides). Headings are never ended by a full stop. Abbreviations are to be avoided in headings.

11.5.1   This first, major heading (and all other centred headings) should be separated from any preceding text by 1.5 line spaces and from the following text by 0.5 line space, as follows:

    1.5 >————
    1. *Introduction*
    0.5 >————

If a centred heading appears at the top of a page, a space of one line (not 1.5 lines) should appear above it.

11.6 *The second level of heading (sub-heading)* is usually ranged left (as a 'shoulder head'). It is italicized in upper and lower case, and capitalized like main headings. It differs from main headings by being preceded by a single line space, without any spacing below it. If numbering the sub-sections will add clarity, the letters a., b., c., etc. (in roman, lower case) are used. Thus:

    1>————
    a. *The Second-Level Heading*
    Text begins here.

11.7 *The third level of heading (sub-sub-heading)* is usually ranged left and preceded by a line space. This heading is also in italics, which may or may not be capitalized. If it is numbered, an Arabic numeral in roman is used, followed by a full stop. The sub-sub-heading is followed by a full stop and the text of the paragraph text runs on immediately. Thus:

    1. *Sub-sub-heading.* Flush left, followed by text on the same line.

11.8 Where a second-level heading comes immediately after a first-level heading, it is separated from it by a space of half a line.

11.9 For a major division between paragraphs in the text, where no heading is required, a one-line space should be left, and the following paragraph should begin flush left. This method of indicating a major division in a chapter should be avoided on the whole, since if it happens that the paragraph after the division begins at the top of a page it is not evident that there has been a major division in the chapter.

11.10   *Running Heads.* The title of the book (or a shorter form of it) constitutes the running head for the left-hand page of each chapter (except the first page). The chapter heading (or a shorter form of it), preceded by the number of the chapter, constitutes the running head for the right-hand page of each chapter (except the first page). Running heads are never ended by a full stop. SAP does not generally use footers or drop folios (numbers at the foot of the page), even when there is no page number in a header, as with the first page of chapters. Page numbers appear at the top left of left-hand pages and the top right of right-hand pages. Abbreviations should be avoided in running heads.

11.11   Running heads should not appear on display pages in front matter or end matter (that is, on the half-title or series title page, title page, bibliographical page, first pages of Contents, Foreword, Preface, Acknowledgments, table of plates, Abbreviations, List of Contributors, Introduction, Appendix, Bibliography, Indexes), or on the Part title, chapter opening, or any page containing *only* an illustration or a table. A page with lines of text as well as an illustration or a table should, however, have a running head. So should the second and following pages of Contents, Abbreviations, Preface, etc.

12. Tables and Other Special Styles

12.1 The following formats or styles should be indicated in the left-hand margin of the manuscript (ringed as for all instructions to typesetters), at the beginning of the new format. A vertical line in the margin indicates the extent of the material to be set in the special format.

i	for indented quotations
p	for poetic lines (which are indented if they spill onto the next line)
bib1	for the author–date type of bibliography (with the date in the left-hand column)
bib2	for the traditional bibliography style
fn	to indicate a new footnote (only if not clear where it begins)
v	for poetry with verse or line numbers to the left-hand side
n	for numbered points that form part of the main text
3 cols. etc.	for tables in columns

12.2 Tables, indented quotations, poetry and verse formats are preceded and followed by a half-line space. In the main text, which is usually set in 14 pt type (for reduction later), they are printed in 12 pt. Indented quotations, tables, etc. are to be avoided in footnotes wherever possible. If it will be clear to the typesetter where such indented matter begins and ends, there is no need to mark the line spacing before and after.

13. VERBAL STYLE

13.1 *'A' and 'an'*. Before an *h* that is pronounced, 'a' rather than 'an' is used. Thus

a historian
a hotel
a harangue
an honour
an *h*
a LXX reading (it is presumed that 'LXX' is pronounced 'Septuagint')

13.2 *Brackets (Parentheses)*. Brackets within brackets are square. The use of brackets is a matter of punctuation that is conformed to our housestyle regardless of how it stands in the original that is being quoted. Even round brackets within the title of a book or article become square brackets inside round brackets; thus

G.H. Jones ('The Decree of Yahweh [Ps. ii 7]', *VT* 15 [1965], pp. 336-44)
(e.g. J. Cheryl Exum, *Fragmented Women: Feminist [Sub]versions of Biblical Narratives*)

The major exception to this rule is that square brackets indicating material inserted into a quotation by the author quoting (as with [*sic*], §13.24) stay in square brackets.

13.3 *'But' at the Beginning of a Sentence*. 'But' or 'Yet' at the beginning of a sentence should not usually be followed by a comma. Nevertheless, the following sentence is correct, since the intervening phrase is rightly separated off from the rest of the sentence by commas before and after it:

But, according to Pfeiffer, this failed.

13.4 *Comma*. Misleading juxtapositions through absence of a comma should be corrected:

not As the eschatological Lord Jesus is presented . . .
but As the eschatological Lord, Jesus is presented . . .

13.5 *Dates.* SAP's housestyle, as a matter of principle, is to use the abbreviations BCE and CE (Before the Common Era, Common Era) with year numbers rather than BC and AD. But the BC, AD style may be used if the author feels strongly about it. Note that both BCE and CE follow the year number. Other styles for dates include:

24 April 1990	during the fifties and
in the 1960s	sixties
the class of '89	13,500 BP (before the
the nineteenth century	present)

13.6 *E.g.* Sentences within the body of the text should never begin with 'e.g.', and 'e.g.' is usually permissible in the body of the text only if it introduces a list or if it is within brackets. A footnote can begin 'e.g.' if the footnote is not a complete sentence:

1. E.g. Smith 1982: 252.
2. For example, Smith (1982: 252) agrees.
3. See, e.g., Smith 1982: 252.

13.7 *Equals.* The equals sign (=) should be used sparingly. For giving translational equivalents, the simple comma is preferable, e.g.

das Mädchen, 'the young girl'

The equals sign (=) is preceded and followed by a space (but there is no space between an opening bracket and an equals sign). The equals sign should not be used as a verb meaning 'equals'.

13.8 *Etc.* is an abbreviation of *et cetera*, 'and other things' (etc. is not italicized, but *et cetera* is italicized if written in full). At the end of a list of persons, write *et al.* (*et alii*, 'and other persons').

13.9 *Festschrift.* The term Festschrift should be used in this form (not in the abbreviation FS) and it should not be in italics.

13.10 *Footnotes to Titles.* A footnote to the title of an article or a chapter is marked with an asterisk, not a footnote number.

13.11 *Foreign Words.* A foreign word in English text should be in italics or (sometimes) in inverted commas, but not both. A general rule is that foreign words that are now part of standard English usage need not be italicized, but it is hard always to know what counts as standard English usage. We italicize *et al.*, *redaktionsgeschichtlich, enfant terrible, Sitz im Leben,* but do not italicize i.e., e.g., per se, contra, etc., vis-à-vis, inter alia. Note that in Section C of this Manual there is a checklist of Spellings, Capitalizations and Abbreviations and Italicizations (§34).

13.12 *'However' at the Beginning of a Sentence.* At the beginning of a sentence 'However' should normally be followed by a comma; within a sentence, it is preceded and followed by a comma.

13.13 *'I' and 'We'.* Copy-editors should change the use of circumlocutions for the first-person singular ('the present writer', 'we', etc.) to 'I'. 'We' is appropriate if it means 'I, the author, and you, the reader'; so 'as we have seen' is usually correct because the author can reasonably assume that the reader has seen what the author has shown; but 'as we have argued' is incorrect, because it is the author, not the reader, who is doing the arguing. Though this is a matter of principle with the Press, the rule is, as with all changes to the author's wording, that if the author is unwilling to accept the Press's style, we accede to the author.

13.14 *'Infer' and 'imply'.* 'Infer' means 'draw an inference, conclusion'; 'imply' means 'put an inference, conclusion into a sentence'. Usually it is authors who imply, readers who infer.

13.15 *Inverted Commas.* Inverted commas are used with a word that is referring to the concept denoted by the word:

> The term 'love' is infrequent.
> We should translate it 'give'.

But in the following it is not the *term* 'love' that is spoken of but the *concept* of love, and so inverted commas are not required:

> Now three things remain, faith: hope and love.

13.16   *Numerals.* numerals are usually written out in full when they are ten or below, when they begin a sentence and when they are an even hundred, thousand, million, etc. But in references, series, tables or large groups or numerals it is better to have consistency than to follow the rule (thus 'He was to wait 7, 14 or 21 days'). The numbers of centuries should always be written out in full: first century, tenth century, etc. Years BCE or BP (Before the Present) have no comma if less than 10,000; thus 6000 BCE, 10,000 BCE, 26,500 BP.

13.17   *Numerals, Roman.* Roman numerals should normally be used only for volume numbers of modern books (numbers of journal issues should be Arabic). Thus

> Strack–Billerbeck, *Kommentar*, II, pp. 295-98
> *TDNT*, IV, p. 230
> but Josephus, *Wars* 2.394
> Chapter 4
> *JBL* 79 (1981).

References to ancient authors should not use Roman numerals (thus 4Q212 3.5; *Baal* 1.2.34-39). But reference to plays should follow the usual format for acts, scenes and lines (thus *King Lear* II.iii.23).

13.18   *Numerals, Separated by Hyphen.* When first and last numbers are separated by a hyphen (e.g. for page references), only the last two digits of the second number should be given, except when the first of the two would then be a zero: thus Jones, pp. 153-79; but Smith, pp. 105-107. The main exception to this rule is with years BCE, where all digits are given, e.g. 590–502 BCE. This is not the case for years CE or AD, e.g. AD 470–90. (Note the use of the en-dash between year numbers, but of the simple hyphen between page numbers.)

13.19   *Only.* 'Only' should always be immediately before the word or phrase it modifies.

13.20   *Page Numbers.* Page numbers are given in the form 'pp. 236-27, 401-405'. The use of 'f.', 'ff.' or *'et seq.'* is avoided as far as possible. Authors are queried at copy-editing stage about any uses they have made of these abbreviations and are asked to clarify the exact extent of the reference being made in each case. In exceptional cases, and only with the agreement of the Managing Editor, 'f.' and 'ff.' may be allowed to stand throughout an entire book.

13.21   *Possessives.* For possessives of proper names ending in a (pronounced) *s* or another sibilant add 's, e.g. Childs's *Introduction*, Jones's views. The exception is for ancient names ending in *s* pronounced (even if not universally) as *z* (Sophocles', Moses', Jesus'; but Josephus's). Write Descartes', Barthes', since the final *s* is not pronounced.

13.22   *'Re'.* This term should not be used except in legal reports. One should not write 'the data re Jerusalem', but 'about', 'concerning'.

13.23   *'Same'.* 'same' should not be used as a mere reference back to a previous noun, as in 'the nature of regional trade, and the degree of centralization of same'. In that sentence, one should replace it by 'that trade'.

13.24   *Sic.* When *sic* is used to signal some error or noteworthy oddity in a quoted passage, the style is [*sic*], i.e. within square brackets (because here the author of our book is inserting a word into the text of the quotation) and in italics. An exclamation mark after *sic* is unnecessary.

13.25   *Singular and Plural.* A block of verses (such as 1.3-5) counts as a single unit; so a singular verb is used, unless the author is explicitly talking about the verses or chapters, e.g.

> 2.1 uses this term, while 2.4-14 lacks it altogether; vv. 2 and 3, on the other hand, have a synonym.

13.26   *Split Infinitives.* It is preferable to avoid split infinitives (e.g. 'to boldly go') when possible, that is, where the adverb can sit equally well either side of the infinitive (it may even go well elsewhere in the clause); but there are occasions when a split infinitive is not only allowable but necessary.

13.27   *Stroke.* A stroke (US slash) usually indicates an *alternative*. So in year dates, for example, write 1969–70, not 1969/70. But financial years (which include only parts of two calendar years) and, likewise, academic years (in the northern hemisphere) are conventionally called 1989/90, etc.

13.28   *'Unique'.* This term is not to be qualified; 'very unique' or 'rather unique' should be simply 'unique'—or else not 'unique' at all.

13.29   *'Versus'.* The word 'versus' is written in full unless imitating the competitive style: Paul vs. Peter, as if it were a boxing match. The form 'vs.' is acceptable in indexes.

13.30   *'Which' and 'that'.* The simplest rule for distinguishing these two relative pronouns is this: 'which' begins a descriptive clause, 'that' a defining clause. 'This is the house that Jack built' *defines* the house as the one built by Jack; 'This is the house which Jack built' *describes* the house further. Another example: 'The police stopped the first car that was driven by a woman' (they were looking for a car driven by a woman); 'The police stopped the first car which was driven by a woman' (the first car that came along happened to be driven by a woman). 'Which' clauses could in principle always be preceded by a comma; they give additional information. 'That' clauses cannot be preceded by a comma because they are an essential part of the definition of their antecedent. It is not always possible for a copy-editor to decide whether the author intends a defining or a descriptive clause; but every example of 'which' and 'that' should be considered; if in doubt, copy-editors should leave the word the author has written.

14. SPELLING

14.1 SAP always uses British spelling, except for books and articles whose author has elected to use American spelling. If there is more than one author in a work, both British and American spelling may be used.

14.2 Any doubts about spelling that are not addressed by this Manual are to be resolved by recourse in the first place to *Collins English Dictionary* and in the second place to the *Oxford English Dictionary* and (in the case of American spellings) to *Webster's College Dictionary.*

14.3 The Press uses the ize ending (one of the standard British spellings), not -ise, except in the case of certain words that must be spelled (in British spelling) with -ise, e.g. advertise, compromise, enterprise, prise, advise, exercise.

14.4 There is in Section C of this Manual a checklist of spellings, capitalizations, abbreviations and italicizations (§34). As far as spellings are concerned, note the following forms as SAP's standards:

> focuses, focused, focusing (*not* focusses, etc.)
> among, while (*not* amongst, whilst)
> with regard to (*not* with regards to)
> first, secondly, *or* first, second (but not *firstly*)
> Muslim (not Moslem)
> *Sitz im Leben* (not hyphenated)
> mediaeval, archaeology, primaeval, Judaean, Matthaean, Galilaean, Maccabaean, Hasmonaean, Graeco-Roman (in British spelling)
> medieval, primeval, etc., but archaeology (in American spelling)
> acknowledgment, judgment, abridgment
> interpretative (but interpretive in American spelling)
> analyse (but analyze in American spelling)

Lukan, Markan
dependant (noun), dependent (adj.)

14.5 The German double s (ß, *Eszett*) is used only in a quotation in German (not, for example, in a German proper name that occurs in an English sentence or as a word in the title of a book or a journal).

14.6 *Biblical Book Names.* In a few cases, more than one name of a biblical book exists; the author's preference is followed. Thus

> Ecclesiastes *or* Qoheleth
> Sirach *or* Ben Sira *or* Ben Sirach *or* Ecclesiasticus
> Song of Songs *or* Canticles

But 'S.' or 'St' with the names of books of the New Testament (e.g. St Matthew, The Epistle of S. Paul to the Romans) is to be avoided. For abbreviations of biblical book names, see Section C of this Manual, §24.2.

14.7 *Hebrew Letters.* The Hebrew letters are spelled aleph (*or* 'aleph), beth, gimel, daleth, he, waw, zayin, ḥeth (*or* heth), ṭeth (*or* teth), yod, kaph, lamedh, mem, nun, samekh, ayin (*or* 'ayin), pe, ṣade (*or* sade), qoph, resh, sin, shin, taw. They are written in roman type. The terms *kethib* and *qere* are thus spelled, and written in italic.

14.8 *Hebrew Grammatical Terms.* The names of the Hebrew verb conjugations (voices, *binyanim*) are spelled thus: qal, niphal, piel, pual, hiphil, hophal, hithpael, polel, polal, etc. (abbreviated qal, ni., pi., pu., hi., ho., htp., pol., polal, etc.).

15. Punctuation

15.1 *Comma.* A comma at the beginning of a phrase or clause should usually be balanced by a closing comma—though not of course if the phrase or clause begins or concludes the sentence. Thus:

> If he spoke, he always suggested.
> He never argued, even if he was right.
> It seems clear that, considering the circumstances, she was justified.
> For a better analysis, see... [a form of words especially common in footnotes].

15.2 A comma should not come between the subject of a sentence and its verb—unless parenthetical material intervenes, e.g.

> The man, who came from France, told me...
> *not* The man who came from France, told me...

15.3 In a series of three of more items, the last item, if connected by 'and', is not preceded by a comma, unless ambiguity would be created otherwise, or unless the items are of unequal length, or unless the author seems to intend a pause, e.g.

> Tom, Dick and Harry
> faith, hope and love
> *but* the trial of faith, the experience of hope, and love
> *and* They had no time to stop, and stare, and listen.

This rule is in disagreement with American practice, which writes 'Tom, Dick, and Harry'; but it is the policy of SAP to use British punctuation even when the work uses American spelling.

15.4 In a series of items in which the comma is needed within particular items, the items themselves can be separated by semicolons. Thus

> She wrote many complex, convoluted papers; seven
> lengthy, difficult books; and a host of breezy, intimate
> letters.

15.5 Before quoted words, a comma is usually the correct punctuation. Thus

> He says, 'You are God's children'.
> *not* He says: 'You are God's children'.

But before an indented quotation a colon is often acceptable.

15.6 *Quotation Marks*. Quotations, whether of single words, phrases or sentences, should be enclosed in single quotation marks. Double quotation marks are used only for quotations within quotations.

15.7 A closing quotation mark comes before the closing punctuation of a sentence unless the sentence began within the quotation. For example,

> Jones maintains that 'there is no case for a "Son of Man"
> title in Judaism. It rests on a misunderstanding.'

15.8 After a question mark or exclamation mark and closing quotation mark, further punctuation is usually unnecessary (though in a bibliographic or footnote entry, the punctuation may well be needed). Thus

> '...and that is how he left it!'
> J.H. Smith, 'Does God Love People?', *Faith* 17 (1977),
>   pp. 10-22.
> Said Cain, 'Are you my brother's keeper?' (Gen. 4.6).
> Was it Cain who said, 'Are you my brother's keeper?'?

15.9 *Brackets*. References to page numbers, biblical texts and the like within a sentence should be enclosed in brackets (US parentheses). Thus

> As Brown remarks (p. 37)...
> The words reappear later (v. 29).

15.10   Brackets within brackets are square (see §13.2 above). But sometimes, so as to avoid brackets within brackets, a comma may be used to introduce a reference of this kind; thus

> The principal characters in this chapter (Moses, 12.1) and
> the next (Aaron, 13.2) ...

15.11 *Verse Numbers* As a rule, verse numbers are separated from one another by a comma, chapter and verse numbers by a full stop, and chapter numbers from one another by a semicolon. But the semicolon should be avoided when the numbers form part of the normal flow of the sentence and the semicolon could consequently be misunderstood as a major punctuation mark for the sentence itself. Thus

> Many psalms have headings (e.g. Pss. 42–49; 84–85; 87–88;
>   95).
> The following psalms have headings: Pss. 42–49, 84–85 and
>   87–88.

15.12 *Colon.* The function of a colon is to introduce a list or other matter that elaborates what precedes:

> These are the requirements for a bishop: temperance,
>   dignity, hospitality ...
> The saying is sure: If anyone desires the office of a
>   bishop ...

A colon may be followed by a capitalized word only if that word begins a complete sentence (or, of course, is a proper noun).

15.13 A colon is not used to separate biblical chapter and verse numbers (a full stop is used instead), nor after the introduction to a quotation in a normal sentence (a comma is used instead; but see §15.5 above). A colon is commonly used to introduce an indented quotation.

15.14 In a table and where the layout shows that certain words are a heading, there is usually no need for colons at the end of the headings.

15.15 *Semicolon.* A semicolon is used between independent clauses in a sentence, that is, between clauses that are not joined by a conjunction. For example,

> The point cannot be proved; evidence is entirely lacking.

15.16   The semicolon can also be used to separate items in a series if the items themselves include commas (see §15.4 above).

15.17   *No Comma.* No comma follows 'i.e.' or 'e.g.', though their full forms ('that is', 'for example') require (contrary to US practice) a following comma. No comma follows 'viz.' nor its full form, 'namely'.

15.18   *Section Mark.* The section or paragraph mark (§) is followed immediately (without a space) by a number or letter.

16. Capitalization

16.1 *Capitalization within Sentences*
The capitalization of words in titles of books and articles is dealt with below (§§16.13-15). In what immediately follows (in §§16.2-15) the issue is capitalization within sentences, whether in the text of a book or article or in footnotes.

16.2 Capitalize Bible, Torah (in reference to the five books of Moses), Scripture, Gospel (in reference to one of the four Gospels), Septuagint(al), Pentateuch(al), Epistles, Jewish, Gentile, Hellenistic, Semitic, Christology, Holy Spirit, the Spirit (in reference to the Holy Spirit), Messiah (when used as a proper name), Psalms (in reference to the book of Psalms), Psalm 23 (etc.), Second Temple.

16.3 Do not capitalize biblical, scriptural, gospel (the preached gospel), christological(ly), messiah (when used as a common noun), messianic, rabbinic, psalm (as in 'many psalms', 'this psalm'), book (as in 'book of Amos').

16.4 Capitalize King David; but David the king, the king of Israel.

16.5 Pronouns referring to God are not capitalized.

16.6 Write 'ancient Near East', not 'Ancient Near East'.

16.7 In Greek, only proper names are capitalized. Even as the first word in an English sentence, a Greek word, even if it is in transliteration, is not capitalized unless it is a proper name.

16.8 Compound (hyphenated) words are capitalized thus: The second element is capitalized if it is a noun, but not if it is a participle modifying the first element or if the compound is a single word. Thus

> Twentieth-Century Literature
> Bird's-Eye and Worm's-Eye Views of Justice
> The Non-Christian Religions
> The Vice-President
> English-speaking Peoples
> The President-elect
> A Re-evaluation
> Tele-ordering

If the first element is capitalized only because it is the first word of the sentence, the second element is not capitalized. Thus

> The Task of a Copy-Editor
> Copy-editors should ...

16.9 Roman page numbers should not be capitalized (even if they are printed as capitals in a publication that is being cited), e.g.

> pp. c-cxi [*not* C-CXI]

16.10 In German, all nouns are capitalized, but no other words except the first in a sentence (e.g. *Zeitschrift für die alttestamentliche Wissenschaft*). But note, exceptionally, *Das Altes Testament, Das Neues Testament*.

16.11 In French, only the first word in a sentence and proper names are capitalized. In the names of institutions and journals only the first noun has a capital:

> l'Académie française
> Revue ecclésiastique

16.12 Capital letters in French do not normally take an accent. However, where the names of authors are given in capitals, in a catalogue, for example, the accent is retained (otherwise, the correct spelling might not be known to the reader).

16.13 *Capitalization in the Titles of Books and Articles*
For capitalization of titles in footnotes, bibliography and elsewhere, the rule is that in English the initial letter of the first word and of all nouns, adjectives, verbs (including auxiliary

verbs) and adverbs should be capitalized but the initial letters of possessive pronouns, prepositions, articles and conjunctions are not, as a rule (note *In Memory of Her* but *In Memory of her Life*). This capitalization should be carried out regardless of the style of capitalization used by the publication being quoted.

16.14　A sentence or part of a sentence that appears in a title is capitalized as a sentence; thus

> '"I have perfumed my bed with myrrh": The Foreign Woman in Proverbs 1–9'

16.15　In the titles of books and articles in other languages, only proper names and the first word of the title and sub-title are capitalized. Note that terms for 'Old Testament' and the like are proper names. Thus

> *Les institutions de l'Ancien Testament*
> *Lexicon in Veteris Testamenti libros*
> *Lezioni di linguistica semitica*

17. ABBREVIATIONS

17.1 For full reference lists of abbreviations in different categories, see §§24-25 below. There will be found lists of abbreviations of the names of biblical books, of the pseudepigrapha and early Christian writings, of the works of Philo and Josephus, of the Dead Sea Scrolls, of the rabbinic writings (Mishnah, Talmud, etc.) and of the Gnostic Nag Hammadi tractates. There also is an extensive list of abbreviations of reference works, periodicals and serials.

17.2 *Abbreviations and Contractions.* Distinguish between abbreviations proper (e.g. Gen., fig., ed.) and contractions (e.g. Jn, Dr). A contraction is a form in which the last letter is the final letter of the word as spelled in full. Abbreviations end with a full stop, contractions without a full stop. The plural of an abbreviation is treated as an abbreviation, even if its last letter is the same as the last letter of the full word (thus eds., figs.). For example:

> Gen., vol., vols., ed., eds., fig., figs., etc.
> Mr, Dr, edn, Jn, Mk, 1 Kgs

17.3 An exception to the above rule is the case of abbreviations of metric measure (e.g., km, m, kg), which never end with a full stop.

17.4 SAP style tends to avoid full stops in acronyms and similar short forms; thus

> SBL, NEH, SNTS, SPCK, SCM, am, pm, PhD

17.5 'That is' and 'for example' should be written out in full in the body of the text unless they precede a list or are within brackets, in which case 'i.e.' and 'e.g.' are to be used. After 'i.e.' and 'e.g.' there is no comma, unless one precedes; after 'viz.' there is no comma. Thus

That is, for example, the cause ... [*not* That is, e.g., the cause]
Some scholars, e.g. Bultmann, Bornkamm, Brown, have argued ...
Some scholars (e.g. Bultmann, Bornkamm, Brown) have argued ...
Some scholars (e.g. Bultmann) have argued ...
Some scholars, for example, Bultmann, have argued ...
See, e.g., Smith 1982: 155 [*not* See, e.g. Smith 1982: 155]

17.6 *Names of Biblical Books.* The names of biblical books are spelled out in full, except when chapter *and* verse number(s) are given; thus Genesis 11, Genesis 11–12, but Gen. 11.1. The exception to this rule is in footnotes and in brackets in the main text, where the abbreviated form is used even if only the chapter number is given. The names of biblical books are not abbreviated in display material, including book and chapter titles, sub-headings, or the Table of Contents.

17.7 *Biblical Chapter and Verse.* The words 'chapter' and 'verse' in biblical references are abbreviated to ch. (plural chs.) and v. (plural vv.), except at the beginning of a sentence, where they are written out in full.

17.8 *Chapter and Verse (etc.) in Other Ancient Sources.* References to books and chapters, etc., in ancient authors use Arabic numerals with a full stop between book and line, chapter and paragraph, etc. Thus Homer, *Iliad* 20.317; Josephus, *Ant.* 5.223. The author's name is followed by a comma, as is normal for modern authors also. The author's name should not be abbreviated; thus

> Aristotle, *Eth.*
> *not* Arist. *Eth.*

There is no comma between the name of the ancient work and the number reference, on the analogy of biblical references (e.g. Gen. 12.21; *Iliad* 20.317).

17.9 *References to the Talmud.* References to the Talmud are always of the form *Ber.* 12a; *Sanh.* 37b (the letters referring to the recto and verso of the page of the standard edition). If there is no indication to the contrary, it can be assumed that the reference is to the Babylonian Talmud. If there are in the vicinity references also to the Palestinian Talmud (also known as the Jerusalem Talmud), it is necessary to distinguish between the Babylonian and Palestinian Talmuds; the forms of citation are *b. Ber.* 12a, *y. Ber.* 12a.

17.10 *References to the Mishnah and Tosefta*. Mishnah references are always of the form *Ber.* 2.1; *Sanh.* 12.2 (i.e. abbreviated tractate name, chapter and verse). Tosefta references have the same form (e.g. *Ber.* 2.1; *Sanh.* 12.2). If it is necessary to distinguish between Mishnah and Tosefta references, the appropriate forms are: *m. Ber.* 2.1, *t. Ber.* 2.1. If *m.* does not precede a reference of this form, it is assumed that it is a reference to the Mishnah.

17.11 *Chapters in Modern Works*. References to the chapters in a modern work should not be abbreviated. The word 'chapter' is capitalized if a number follows. Chapters are always referred to with Arabic numerals, even if, for design reasons, the number of the chapter may be spelled out at the head of the chapter proper, e.g. 'CHAPTER THREE'. Thus

> In Chapter 3 I will show; in the last chapter.

17.12 *Figures*. When a Figure or a Plate is referred to in the text, it is usual to spell the word 'Figure' or 'Plate' out in full (though if the term is to be much repeated, it is better to abbreviate it). In a reference within brackets, the abbreviated form 'Fig.' or 'Pl.' should be used. As the title to a figure, the abbreviated form is used. When a figure has smaller elements, write, for example, Fig. 12a (*not* 12:a), or Fig. 7.15. For example,

> In Figure 2 there is set out ...
> In Fig. 1 there is a list of dates, in Fig. 3 a map, in Fig. 4 a chart ...
> (see Fig. 2)
> Fig. 2 Location of Sites
> Pl. 6 View from the Air

17.13 *Measurements.* After numbers, a unit of measurement should be abbreviated in more technical material but spelled out in more literary contexts. For example,

> Jerusalem, c. 23 m. NW of Jericho …
> Jerusalem is more than 20 kilometres from the Dead Sea.

There is a space between the numeral and the unit, thus 23 km, not 23km.

17.14 *Not to Be Abbreviated.* The words University and Professor are never abbreviated (contrariwise, Dr as an academic title is never spelled out).

17.15 *Abbreviations without Full Stops.* Degrees, honours and ecclesiastical orders are without a full stop, e.g. MA, PhD, DPhil, OBE, SJ, OP. So too are abbreviations of United States state names, e.g. CA, AZ, PA, CT, DC.

17.16 *Abbreviations in Small Caps.* Abbreviations for Bible versions (e.g. KJV, AV, RSV, NRSV) and for eras (e.g. BCE, BC, CE, AD) are written in small caps, and without full stops.

17.17 *Abbreviations of Hebrew Terms.* The names of the Hebrew verb conjugations (voices, *binyanim*) are abbreviated thus: qal, ni., pi., pu., hi., ho., htp., pol., polal, etc. The abbreviated form is typically used after a Hebrew verb is cited, thus

> The hiphil of שׂכל usually has the sense …
> Verbs with this sense are: שׂכל hi., חכם htp., etc.

17.18 *Common Abbreviations.* Following is a list of some commonly used abbreviations.

AAR (American Academy of Religion)
ad loc. (in the appropriate place)
a m
B A
c. (not ca.), *circa* (about)
cf.
cu. in.
Dr
e.g.
esp.
etc.
Fig.

ft (foot, feet)
i.e.
ibid.
in., ins. (inch, inches)
Jr (Junior)
kg
lit.
m (metre)
m. (mile)
m² (square metre)
M A
MLA (Modern Languages
    Association)
Mr
n.p. (no place name given)
NE
NEH (National Endowment
    for the Humanities)
NS (New Series)
NW
NY (New York state)

op. cit. [but its use is to be
    avoided]
OS (Old Series)
PhD
Pl. (Plate)
p m
q.v. (which see)
Revd
s.v. (*sub verbo*)
SBL (Society of Biblical
    Literature)
SE
SNTS (Societas Novi
    Testamenti Studiorum)
SOTS (Society for Old
    Testament Study)
sq. in.
St
SW
UK
US, USA

A fuller Checklist of Spellings, Capitalizations, Abbreviations and Italicizations can be found in §34 below.

18. Quotations

18.1 *Quotation Marks.* For the position of quotation marks, see §15.6-8.

18.2 *Form of Quotations.* Quotations should follow the exact form of the original, including, for example, spellings, punctuation and the style of citation for biblical texts even if they deviate from SAP housestyle. Any material inserted into the quotation by the author citing the material is to be included within square brackets, round brackets (parentheses) being reserved for parenthetical material within the quotation itself.

18.3 *Indented Quotations.* Indented quotations (12 pt in the proofs of the main text, which is about 9 pt in the printed text) are used for any quotations over four lines or 40 words. But this rule is not applied rigidly. For example, if an author is making three quotations in order to compare the views of three scholars, it would be wrong not to print them all in the same format even if one of them had fewer than 40 words. Indented quotations may also be used (occasionally) for smaller sections of material that is being highlighted, including one or two lines of poetry.

18.4 Indented quotations, like tabular matter, are to be avoided in footnotes whenever possible.

18.5 If an indented quotation ends with a reference to its source, the reference is in brackets, and the closing punctuation usually falls outside the brackets, e.g.

> To be or not to be, that is the question (*Hamlet* IV.ii.2).
> *but* Where is your steadfast love of old? (Ps. 89.49).

18.6 *Ellipses.* Ellipses (three spaced full stops, or the typesetting character …) have spaces on either side. It is not usually correct to indicate any other punctuation when ellipses are used. Thus if a quoted sentence is abbreviated at a comma, only the ellipsis mark is needed (...); the form ', ...' is usually wrong. When a quotation ends with an ellipsis, it is as if it ended with a full stop; so no punctuation is required after the closing quotation mark. Thus

> Rachel said, 'You have wronged me...'

18.7   All quotations are in the nature of things an extract from a longer text, so ellipses should not be used simply to indicate that in the original text there are preceding and following words. The marks of ellipsis should be reserved for occasions when it is specially necessary to draw attention to that fact, or when the words quoted are self-evidently syntactically incomplete.

18.8   *Quotations of Greek and Hebrew.* Quotations of Greek and Hebrew are not marked with quotation marks, since their alphabets suffice to indicate that words are being quoted.

19. HYPHENS AND DASHES

19.1 There are four types of hyphen and dash: the hyphen proper (or hard hyphen, §19.2-6), the soft hyphen (§19.7-9), the en-dash (§19.10) and the em-dash (§19.11).

19.2 *The Hard Hyphen.* The hyphen proper (-) is used to break or join words, as in anti-disestablishmentarianism, right-hand margin, nineteenth-century scholarship. It is also used between page numbers, verse numbers, line numbers, volume and issue numbers: pp. 1-17, vv. 10-20, etc. Certain *compounds* require a hyphen: one-inch margin, three-year interval, one-year-old child, 14-feet-thick wall. But the correct forms are: 10 per cent increase, 4 m thick wall, since per cent is never hyphenated, nor are abbreviations of metric measures.

19.3 *Hyphen in Compound Words.* Some examples of the use of the hyphen in compound words follow. For further examples, see the *Chicago Manual of Style*, pp. 176-81. *Collins English Dictionary* should be consulted for difficult examples.

> *with a prefix, to separate two identical vowels*: pre-existing, pre-empt, re-emphasized, re-excavated, re-evaluation, pre-exilic, anti-imperialist, semi-independent (*but* cooperative, cooperate)
>
> *(occasionally) with a prefix, to separate two identical consonants*: inter-regional, non-national
>
> *to separate a prefix from a capitalized noun or adjective*: anti-Hellenistic, pro-Jewish, post-Freudian, non-Davidic (also non-biblical)
>
> *to distinguish a compound word from a homonym*: re-cover, re-creation
>
> *to show which words in a chain of nouns and adjectives are most closely linked*: higher-level synthesis, site-size data, one-sided view, nineteenth-century development, high-quality workmanship (*but* high confidence-levels)

19.4 Examples of compound words that are not hyphenated are:

underused	postexilic
sociopolitical	microenvironments
macroeconomics	interdependence
infrastructure	

19.5 There is usually no hyphen between an adverb modifying an adjective or participle and the adjective or participle, thus

loosely linked categories
highly esteemed author
newly discovered data

19.6 The exception is in the case of adverbs that do not end with *-ly* and that have the same form as an an adjective, since they could be mistaken for the adjective, e.g.

a well-known author
a still-active scholar

19.7 *The Soft Hyphen.* All the foregoing are examples of 'hard' hyphens (i.e. hyphens that form part of the spelling of the word). 'Soft' hyphens are those that are used for dividing words at the end of lines.

19.8 *Rules for Soft Hyphenation.* When words are divided by a hyphen at the end of a line, they are divided at the end of a syllable (the Microsoft Word program suggests word divisions that are usually acceptable). Words with syllables of one letter should not be divided after the one letter syllable; thus *reli-able,* not *relia-ble* (but *perme-able* is permissible). A hyphen after the second letter of a word (as is normally proposed by the hyphen- ation program of Microsoft Word) should normally be rejected when the first two letters are not a prefix, so *ad-dress* is usually not acceptable, but *un-ethical* is. The hyphenation of names and proper nouns is permissible, and the option 'Hyphenate Capital- ized Words' in Word's hyphenation program should be selected; but the hyphenation of capitalized words should be accepted only when a line is obviously rather loose.

19.9 The rules about soft hyphens given in §19.8 are not absolute; the priority should be given to the look of the page rather than to the observance of rules. Thus a loose line (with excessive space between words, or, worse still, space between letters) should be avoided at almost any cost (e.g. hyphenating *address*), while ending more than three successive lines with a hyphen or ending a paragraph with only the second half of a hyphenated word are equally undesirable.

19.10 *The en-dash.* The en-dash (–) is used to join otherwise separate elements, such as names (e.g. Ezra–Nehemiah, Luke–Acts), chapters (e.g. chs. 1–3, Jn 1.1–2.10), and year dates (e.g. 1940–45). The en-dash is to be used between all numbers except verse numbers, line numbers, page numbers and volume and issue numbers. An en-dash is also used when the first element does not modify the second. Thus Jewish–Christian tension (tension between Jews and Christians), but Jewish-Christian author (an author who is both Jewish and Christian).

19.11 *The em-dash.* The em-dash (—) is a strong punctuation mark, beginning and/or ending a parenthetical statement within a sentence. Unless the parenthetical statement is at the very end of the sentence, the opening em-dash must be balanced by a closing em-dash (just as would be necessary if the punctuation used were a comma or a bracket).

20. BIBLIOGRAPHY

20.1 For books and articles cited in the Bibliography, it is required that authors should supply as complete publication information as is possible. Publication information includes the place and name of the publishing house, the complete page numbers of articles (even if reference is being made only to certain pages within the article), subtitles of books, series in which books are published, the name of the translator, etc. The capitalization and punctuation of the title of an article or book and of series names are conformed to SAP style (see under Capitalization, §16); everything else is reproduced exactly as it is found in the original source, even if this differs from SAP style. The reasons for conforming capitalization and punctuation to SAP style are (1) for the sake of consistency in the appearance of the Bibliography, and (2) because titles of books are normally set in display type, often without appropriate punctuation, so that it is not always possible to determine what the original edition intends the punctuation or capitalization to be.

20.2 *Books Cited in Bibliography.* The order of data in bibliographic information is the following (the form of the data is shown in brackets in the first column, and the proper punctuation is indicated in the second column):

Element of Bibliography	*followed by*
author(s), editor(s) (ed., eds.)	comma
title	opening round bracket
Festschrift dedicatee (e.g. Festschrift M. Noth)	semicolon
editor (ed.) (if there is an editor as well as an author)	semicolon
translator (trans.)	semicolon
series	comma
number in series	semicolon
number of volumes (e.g. 2 vols.)	semicolon
reprint status (repr.)	comma

place of publication	colon
publisher	comma
edition (e.g. 2nd edn, rev. edn)	comma
date	closing round bracket, full stop

20.3 Not all of these elements are appropriate for every book, of course, but the above is the order in which they should appear if they do exist. Books published before the nineteenth century frequently do not carry a publisher's name. Variations for bibliographies in the author–date system (sometimes known as the social-science style) are noted in §22.6.

20.4 *Articles and Chapters Cited in Bibliography.* Examples of Bibliography entries for articles and chapters in books are as follows:

> Brown, C., 'The "Son of Man" Debate', *NTS* 12 (1970), pp. 121-38.

> Hamerton-Kelly, R., and R. Scroggs (eds.), *Jews, Greeks and Christians: Religious Cultures in Late Antiquity* (Festschrift W.D. Davies; trans. J. Smith; SJLA, 21; Leiden: E.J. Brill, 2nd edn, 1976).

> Martyn, J.L., 'Have we Found Elijah?', in Hamerton-Kelly and Scroggs (eds.), *Jews, Greeks and Christians*, pp. 181-219.

20.5 *Author's Name.* The names of authors who are cited should be given in Bibliographies (as also in footnotes) in the form they themselves use (e.g. John X. Smith, A. Brown, III). The Press is dependent upon its authors for such information, and does not undertake to acquire information with which it has not been supplied. Some authors use only initials for the names of the authors they cite, and it is acceptable to retain that system. Nevertheless, it is the Press's principle that authors should be referred to by the form of name that they themselves prefer.

20.6 *Orders, etc.* Whether or not a religious order to which an author belongs is noted in a bibliography is at the discretion of the SAP author; preferably, the form of name used by the author being cited should be adopted. As far as SAP is concerned, both the following forms are acceptable, but consistency must be maintained throughout:

Vaux, R. de, OP, *Les institutions de l'Ancien Testament*
or Vaux, R. de, *Les institutions de l'Ancien Testament*
Miller, Patrick D., Jr, *Genesis 1–11: Studies in Structure and Theme*
or Miller, Patrick D., *Genesis 1–11: Studies in Structure and Theme*

20.7 *Format of Author's Name.* The format of an author's name in a Bibliography is: Smith, Alfred K. For a multi-authored work (or a work edited by more than one person), the format is:

Smith, Alfred K., Mary Jones and Jane P. Isaacs
Smith, Alfred K., Mary Jones and Jane P. Isaacs (eds.)

For more than three authors or editors, it is permissible to use *et al.*, thus

Smith, Alfred K., *et al.*

20.8 No space separates initials, but there is a space between the last initial and the surname, e.g. A.B. Jones.

20.9 *Multiple Entries.* Multiple entries for an author may be arranged either in chronological or in alphabetical order, but the same principle should be used throughout the Bibliography. When there is more than one work by the same author, the second and subsequent entries begin with a em-dash (—), with no following space. An author's name should sometimes be repeated—for example, when the person is both author and editor of works, or when another person participates in the authorship or editing. Thus:

Smith, A.B., *Life in the Ruhr* (Berlin: de Gruyter, 1972).
—*Life in Ancient Germany* (Berlin: Töpelmann, 1988).
Smith, A.B. (ed.), *Collected Essays on Life in Germany* (Berlin: Töpelmann, 1994)
— *More Collected Essays on Life in Germany* (Berlin: Töpelmann, 1994)
Smith, A.B., and C.A. Charles, *Life in Modern Germany* (Berlin: de Gruyter, 1989).

Smith, A.B., and C.A. Charles (eds.), *An Encyclopaedia of Life in Modern Germany* (Berlin: de Gruyter, 1989).
— *A New Encyclopaedia of Life in Modern Germany* (Berlin: de Gruyter, 1996).

20.10 *Editor's Name.* The name of the editor or editors should be given for works of multiple authorship, e.g. encyclopaedias, volumes of collected essays. Following the names of the editors is (ed.) or (eds.). When a book is cited with an author's name, it is normal that an editor's name is not mentioned (even though, in the case of books published in series, there is usually an editor as well as an author). Exceptional cases are when a book has been substantially revised or rewritten by an editor, who thereby participates in the role of author, or when a classic text is edited with an introduction. Thus

Heinrich Böll, *Bilder eines Lebens* (ed. Hans Scheurer; Cologne: Kiepenhauer & Witsch, 1997).
Lancelot Andrews, *Selected Writings* (ed. P.E. Hewison; Manchester: Carcanet, 1997).

It would be equally acceptable, in the case of the second example, to write

P.E. Hewison (ed.), *Lancelot Andrews: Selected Writings* (Manchester: Carcanet, 1997).

since it could well be argued that Lancelot Andrews never wrote a work entitled *Selected Writings*.

20.11 *Date of Publication.* The date used in bibliographic data is the copyright date of the original edition or of any subsequent edition that is being cited; the date of a reprint (that is, of an unaltered re-edition of the work) should not be given. In the case of two-volume works, the years of publication should be separated by a comma and space (e.g. 1969, 1971), and in the case of multi-volume works the years of publication should be separated by an en-dash (e.g. 1969–75). If only the date of the reprint is known write (for example) 'repr. 1977'. If the reprint is published by a publisher other than the original publisher, 'repr.' comes before the place of publication and the publisher's name.

20.12 *Title and Subtitle.* Between the title and subtitle of a book there is a colon, not a full stop (though occasionally a book has a more complicated title, and a full stop may be appropriate). This format is to be used for subtitles in any language. The subtitle begins with a capital letter. On the title page of printed books there is generally no punctuation between the main title and the subtitle, since the words are set out in display type rather than as a bibliographic entry. So some transformation of the original publication is necessary, and it is SAP's convention to use the semicolon between the main title and the subtitle.

20.13   *Book Series Name.* A series name is followed by a comma and the number in the series. A full stop is used to separate major and minor numbers, e.g. WUNT, 2.1.

20.14   *Volume Number.* A volume number (but not the number of volumes, e.g. 2 vols.) for a modern work is in Roman numerals. When a page number is also specified, the volume number is followed by a comma before the page number (preceded by p. or pp. in traditional style but not in author–date style), e.g.

> *TDNT*, III, p. 123 [not vol. 3]
> Jones 1982: II, 565

20.15   *Place of Publication.* Recognized English spellings of foreign cities are to be used: thus Cologne, Munich, Moscow, The Hague, Rome. But note that some places retain their foreign-language spellings in English, e.g. Münster, Göttingen, Zürich. See also the extensive list of publishers' names and places of publication in §27.

20.16   *More than One Place of Publication.* When a publisher has more than one office, only the first stated or the one presumed to be the head office is noted as the place of publication in the Bibliography and footnote references (see the list of Publishers' Names in Section C of this Manual [§27] for the correct place of publication of many publishers in biblical studies).

20.17   *State, County and Country Names.* The general rule is that names of states of the United States, of counties in England

and Wales, and of countries are included after the place of publication for cities that would not normally be well known by scholars in the discipline. It is, of course, a matter of opinion whether a place of publication is well known. For the sake of consistency, SAP has made a set of decisions on the issue, and the List of Publishers in Section C of this Manual (§27) shows, in the case of most publishers who will be referred to in monographs on the Bible, which places of publication need to be followed by the name of the state, county or country. States of the United States are abbreviated with two letters in capitals (e.g. CA, PA, NY), and the names of other countries are written out in full (e.g. Hamilton, New Zealand). Cambridge, MA, should always be so designated, in order to distinguish it from Cambridge (England).

20.18 *Publisher's Name.* The name of a publisher includes 'Press' if it is part of the name, but not terms denoting the legal status of the company, such as Ltd or Co. or Inc. (except where listed in §27). For the correct form of the name of most publishers of scholarly books in biblical studies, see the list of Publishers' Names in Section C of this Manual (§27).

20.19 *More than One Publisher.* Where a book has been published by more than one publisher, the place and publisher of each edition is given if our author has supplied the information. Thus,

> Exeter: Paternoster Press; Grand Rapids: Eerdmans.

If the years of publication are different, the format is, for example:

> Exeter: Paternoster Press, 1969; Grand Rapids: Eerdmans, 1970.

20.20 *Journal Series.* Some journals have been issued in more than one series; the *Journal of Theological Studies*, for example, published vols. 1-50 in 1900–1949, and began a new series of volumes in 1950; *Jewish Quarterly Review* published vols. 1-20 in 1888–1908 and began a new series in 1910. In such cases, NS in small capitals should be used for volumes in the New Series, whether or not the author has noted the fact; thus

John Smith, 'Hebron', *JTS* NS 21 (1970), pp. 1-8.

The notation OS for Old Series does not generally need to be used. *The Expositor* has several series, which should be referred to in the form: *The Expositor*, First Series 12 (1890), pp. 1-20.

20.21   *Issue Number.* For a journal that paginates its issues continuously through the year (e.g. *Journal of Biblical Literature*, *Vetus Testamentum*, *New Testament Studies* and many major scholarly journals), the issue number should not be given, only the volume number. When each issue number in a volume is separately paginated, the volume number and the issue number should be separated by a full stop; thus

Bible Today 25.2 (1992), pp. 1-12

20.22   *Journal or Book?* Some journals and other serials sometimes bear the marks of a book. This is especially noticeable with *Supplements to Vetus Testamentum*, *Oudtestamentische Studiën* and *Semeia*. The general rule to follow is that if the book bears a book-like title, it is to be treated as a book; the name of the journal or serial is then treated as the name of a book series, which is set in roman type. If there is no book-like title, the serial is treated as a journal. Thus, for example

M. Noth and D. Winton Thomas (eds.), *Wisdom in Israel and in the Ancient Near East, Presented to Professor Henry Harold Rowley...in Celebration of his Sixty-Fifth Birthday* (VTSup, 3; Leiden: E.J. Brill, 1955).

G.I. Davies, 'Megiddo in the Period of the Judges' in *Crises and Perspectives: Studies in Ancient Near Eastern Polytheism, Biblical Theology, Palestinian Archaeology and Intertestamental Literature* (OTS, 24; Leiden: E.J. Brill, 1986), pp. 43-53.

J. Simons, 'The "Table of Nations" (Gen. x): Its General Structure and Meaning", *OTS* 10 (1954), pp. 155-84.

Vernon K. Robbins (ed.), *The Rhetoric of Pronouncement* (Semeia, 64; Atlanta: Scholars Press, 1994).

20.23 *Page Numbers.* Page numbers are preceded by p. or pp., following a comma and space, except in author–date style where the page number follows a colon after the date of publication (§22.2). But even in author–date style, if a page number appears on its own (that is, without a year-date), p. or pp. is to be used.

20.24 *Column Numbers.* Certain journals and books number their columns, rather than their pages. Among the most frequently cited are *Theologische Literaturzeitung* and *Theologisches Handwörterbuch zum Alten Testament*. Col. and cols. must be used in these cases rather than p. and pp., of course.

20.25 *Reprint.* If an article or chapter is known to have been reprinted in an author's collected works or some other editor's collection, the fact may be indicated in brackets after the page numbers, with the same kind and order of information as a normal bibliographic entry. For example,

> James Barr, 'Philology and Exegesis', in C. Brekelmans (ed.), *Questions disputées d'Ancien Testament: Méthode et théologie* (BETL, 33; Gembloux: J. Duculot, 1974), pp. 39-61 (reprinted in James Barr, *Comparative Philology and the Text of the Old Testament, with Additions and Corrections* [Winona Lake, IN: Eisenbrauns, 1987], pp. 362-87).

20.26 *Book Review.* When a book review is an item in the Bibliography, the reviewer's name comes first, then 'review of', then the title of the book and accompanying bibliographical information, then 'by' followed by the author's name; thus

> Jeffrey T. Reed, review of *Paul, the Apostle to America: Cultural Trends and Pauline Scholarship* (Louisville: Westminster/John Knox Press, 1994), by Robert Jewett, in *JSNT* 63 (1996), pp. 125-26.

Note that quotation marks are not used.

20.27 The Bibliographic form, with the author's surname capitalized, is used as the heading for Booklist entries in SAP Journals such as *JSOT*, *JSNT* and *JSP*.

21. Footnotes

21.1 This section refers only to footnotes of the conventional style. For forms of reference using the author–date system, see §22.

21.2 *Authors' Names.* The form of bibliographic citations in footnotes is the same as in the Bibliography (§20), with one exception: in footnotes, authors' forenames or initials precede their surnames. Thus a footnote may begin

> Cf. Alfred K. Smith
> So Alfred K. Smith, Mary Jones and Jane Isaacs ...

For four or more authors, use *et al.* with no preceding punctuation, e.g.

> Alfred K. Smith *et al.*

No space separates initials, but there is a space between the last initial and the surname, e.g. A.B. Jones.

21.3 *Footnote Style for a Book.* Major elements in data about books are separated by semicolons or colons or commas, and all publication data are in brackets (see also §20.2), e.g.

> A.B. Jones, *Matthew* (JSNTSup, 24; Sheffield: JSOT Press, 2nd edn, 1984), p. 123.

21.4 *Footnote Style for a Multi-Volume Work.* One volume of a multi-volume work is cited thus (note that the volume number is in roman not in italics, but the main title and the sub-title are in italics):

> J.H. Charlesworth (ed.), *The Old Testament Pseudepigrapha.* I. *Apocalyptic Literature* (London: Darton, Longman & Todd, 1986).

21.5 *Footnote Style for a Chapter in a Collected Work.* A chapter in a collected work is cited thus:

> J.L. Martyn, 'Have we Found Elijah?', in R. Hamerton-Kelly and R. Scroggs (eds.), *Jews, Greeks and Christians: Religious Cultures in Late Antiquity* (Festschrift W.D. Davies; trans. J. Smith; SJLA, 21; Leiden: E.J. Brill, 2nd edn, 1976), pp. 181-219.

The word 'in' is used to separate the title of an article from the collected work in which it appears, in order to avoid confusion regarding authorship. It is not needed for dictionaries and other standard reference works that collect articles (e.g. *TDNT*, *IDB*, etc.). A chapter by another author in such a collected work should be accompanied at its first occurrence by a full citation of the work.

21.6 *Footnote Style for a Journal Article.* A journal article is cited thus:

> C. Brown, 'The "Son of Man" Debate', *NTS* 12 (1970), pp. 121-38 (125).

Full page numbers should be given for all articles that are cited. The principle is that it is the *article* that is cited, not just the page. If a specific page is being referred to, the page number is put within brackets.

21.7 *Short Titles.* When a book, a chapter or an article is referred to again, after its first occurrence, a short title form is used, thus:

> Jones, *Matthew.*
> Martyn, 'Have we Found Elijah?'
> Brown, 'The "Son of Man" Debate'.

Ibid. and *op. cit.* should not be used. *Idem* may be used only when several works by one author are cited sequentially in a single footnote.

21.8 *Reference to Notes.* If reference is being made to a foot-note, the form is

> p. 23 n. 4
> p. 44 nn. 5, 7
> p. 55 note [if the footnote is not numbered]

21.9 *Bibliographic Reference in a Footnote Sentence.* Both the following forms are acceptable:

Samuel Terrien, *Job: Poet of Existence* (Indianapolis: Bobbs–Merrill, 1957), p. 156, exposits such a reading.

Samuel Terrien *(Job: Poet of Existence* [Indianapolis: Bobbs–Merrill, 1957], p. 156) exposits such a reading.

22. AUTHOR–DATE STYLE
('Social Science' Style)

22.1 The function of the author–date style of references is to reduce the need for footnotes, by embedding references to cited works in the text in abbreviated form (e.g. Brown 1980: 123). SAP's experience is that its authors of monographs and journal articles tend to use footnotes for more than mere reference to works cited: a typical footnote includes extra material not suitable for the main text, or comments on the views of other authors cited in the footnote. So the author–date system is rarely the more appropriate system of notation.

22.2 *In the text*, the basic forms of reference in the author–date style are:

> (Brown 1980)
> (Brown 1980c)
> (Brown 1980: 23-25)
> (Brown 1980: 230 n. 2)
> (Brown 1980: Pl. 10)
> (Brown 1980: Ch. 3)
> (Brown 1980: II, 231).
> (Brown 1980: vol. 2) [if the whole volume is being referred to]
> (BDB, 61) [no colon is used when no date is given]

22.3 Note that there is no punctuation after the author's name and a space always follows the colon between the date and the page reference (which omits 'p.' or 'pp.').

22.4 Several works by the same author are cited by date only, the dates being separated by commas; when page numbers are given, the year dates are separated by semicolons:

> (Jones 1963, 1972a, 1986)
> (Jones 1963a: 10; 1972; 1986: 123)
> (Jones 1963a; 1972a: 156; Smith 1982)

22.5 *In Footnotes.* Footnotes may be used in author–date style, especially if there is too much material to include conveniently within the text without breaking up its flow. The first example below shows the form of the footnote if it contains only author–date references, the second if the author–date reference is included in a sentence:

> Smith 1982: 145; Jones 1980: 68; Clinebell 1968: 85; Taylor 1988: 55.
> Smith (1982: 145) should be consulted for details.

22.6 *In Bibliography.* In the Bibliography, the basic forms of the author–date style are illustrated here:

> Jones, A.
> 1963 *On Consistency* (Harvard Bibliographic Series, 9; 2 vols.; Cambridge, MA: Harvard University Press, 2nd edn).
> 1980 *Second Thoughts on Consistency* (Cambridge: Cambridge University Press).
> 1986a 'Second Thoughts: An Addendum', *Journal of Bibliographic Research* 30: 12-21.
> 1986b 'Second Thoughts: A Further Addendum', *Journal of Bibliographic Research* 30: 332-45.
> Green, W.S. (ed.)
> 1980 *Approaches to Ancient Judaism* (BJS, 9; Chico, CA: Scholars Press).
> Lichtenberg, H., and P. Smith
> 1980 'Atonement and Sacrifice in the Qumran Community', in W.S. Green (ed.), *Approaches to Ancient Judaism* (BJS, 9; Chico, CA: Scholars Press): 159-71 [if this is the only article cited from this volume].
> Lichtenberg, H., and P. Smith
> 1980 'Atonement and Sacrifice in the Qumran Community', in Green 1980: 159-71 [if more than one article is cited from the volume, the volume is listed under the editor's name as in the entry *s.v.* Green above].
> Charlesworth, James H. (ed.)
> 1983, 1985 *The Old Testament Pseudepigrapha* (2 vols.; London: Darton, Longman & Todd).

22.7 The order of entries is by year; if there is more than one item from the same year, the dates are labelled a, b, c, etc. (e.g. 1963a, 1963b).

23. INDEXES

23.1 This chapter concerns the structure and format of indexes. For rules on the procedures for indexing, see Section C of this Manual (§35). On the matter of who should prepare the indexes, and when, consult Section A of this Manual (§4.16).

23.2 *Format of Indexes.* There is no standard format for the indexes of a book. The special character of each book has to be borne in mind when planning its indexes. For most monographs in biblical studies, however, it is usually desirable to have at least two indexes, one of authors cited, and one of biblical passages referred to. Whether there should also be an index of subjects is generally a matter to be decided between the author and the desk editor; it should be noted, however, that the Press cannot undertake to provide subject indexes, and an author who desires to have such an index must be wholly responsible for its preparation (marking on a copy of a proof the forms to be indexed and providing a list of index entries). Some books require an index of non-biblical ancient writings (whether as an independent index or as an appendage to the biblical references index). An author who desires such an index, or whose book requires such an index in the opinion of the Press, must expect to liaise closely with the Press in the preparation of that index, since specialist knowledge of the sources, which cannot necessarily be presumed of the Press's indexers, is often required.

23.3 *Page References.* In indexes, it is not the Press's custom to distinguish between continued discussion of a subject (often indexed, for example, as pp. 30-33), and a number of incidental references to a subject (often indexed as pp. 30, 31, 32, 33) (the distinction is observed by the *Chicago Manual of Style*, §18.9). SAP indexers write 'pp. 30-33' in both cases. However, if an author is embedding index entries in the text of a book (§35) and wishes to distinguish between incidental and continued reference, the automatic indexing procedure allows one to do so (consult the *User's Guide to Microsoft Word 5.0*, p. 535). *Passim* may be used in indexes to indicate very many references throughout the book.

23.4 *What is Indexed.* The Press's rule is that all references to the Bible or other literature are indexed, whether or not the passage is discussed in the text or the footnotes. (But if an author desires to and is willing to make a selection of the references to be indexed, the Press has no objection to that.) In the author index, only the names of authors are indexed, not those of editors, translators and the like (except in the case of a work for which no author's name but only an editor's name is given). In a subject index, an indexer should aim at making no more than two or three entries per page; it is customary to index all proper names as well as important topics in such an index.

23.5 *What is Not Indexed.* The Preface is not usually indexed—at least, not if, as is usually the case, it is an account of how the book came to be written. But if the Preface is more like an Introduction, concerning the subject matter of the book itself, it is to be indexed. The footnotes or endnotes should be indexed exactly as the text is; there is no need to indicate that the reference is to a footnote. The Bibliography should not be indexed.

23.6 *Layout of Indexes.* In subject and author indexes, the subject or author cited is followed by a space and then the page numbers on which the reference appears. In indexes of biblical references, the chapter and verse numbers are followed by a tab, and then the page numbers on which the reference appears.

23.7 *Cross-Headings and Column Headings.* Cross-headings run across the whole page, and so across the two or three columns of the index; column headings are confined to their own column. So, for example, there may be in the References Index a section for the Pseudepigrapha. Whether the Pseudepigrapha will deserve a cross-heading all to themselves will depend upon how many references there are.

23.8 A cross-heading should be in small caps (e.g. PSEUD-EPIGRAPHA). Major column headings should also be in small caps, but most headings within columns should be in italics. Thus under a cross-heading 'RABBINIC AND OTHER JEWISH LITERA-TURE' there may be several column headings such as 'BABYLO-NIAN TALMUD', 'TOSEFTA', 'MIDRASHIM' and the like, and under 'BABYLONIAN TALMUD' the names of various tractates of the Talmud cited, in italics.

23.9 *Author Index*
The surname comes first, followed by a comma, and then the initials of the first names (not the forenames, even if they are given in the book proper). Initials are not separated by spaces. All the initials of an author are given in the Index.

23.10   *Names Beginning with Particles.* The rule for names beginning with particles such as de, von, etc., is this: when the author is English-speaking, the particle comes first, e.g. Van Seters, J., De Vries, S.J. (even if the particle has a lower-case letter). If the author is not English-speaking, the particle usually follows the name, e.g. Vaux, R. de. The main exception is that in French, when the particle consists of the article or a compound of the article it precedes the surname proper (thus Le Déaut, R.; Du Bellay, J.; in the case of La Fontaine, J. de, the article and the preposition are separate, so only the article precedes the surname proper). Further details may be found in Butcher, *Copy-Editing*, p. 136.

23.11   *Compound Personal Names.* Compound personal names should be indexed under the first element of the surname, e.g. Winton Thomas, D., Henton Davies, G. (but note that there are different views on whether such names in English are truly compound; some prefer Thomas, D.W.) Note that in Spanish, however, compound personal names are customary, e.g. Alonso Schökel, L., Díez Macho, A.

23.12   *Alphabetization.* Mac, Mc and M' are indexed purely alphabetically. Malbon precedes McKnight, for example. A letter with an accent sorts after a letter without.

23.13   *Biblical References and Other Ancient Texts Indexes.* References to biblical and other ancient works should be arranged in this order, though some variations are permitted on the basis of the particularities of the book:

Old Testament
Apocrypha (sometimes included with Old Testament)
New Testament
Pseudepigrapha
Qumran
Targums
Mishnah
Talmuds
Tosefta
Midrashim [pl. of Midrash]
Philo
Josephus
Other Jewish Authors
Christian Authors
Other Ancient Authors (or Classical Authors) or Other
     Ancient Sources

23.14   Which of these categories will be used in any particular book depends on the number of items occurring in any one category; for example, if there is only one classical author and several ancient Christian and Jewish ones, there might be a heading ANCIENT AUTHORS, which would include both Christian and Classical. But if there are many in both categories, there might be separate headings.

23.15   Each biblical text (and in most cases, each ancient work) cited has its name given in full as a column heading and in italics (even though it may be cited in the text in roman, as with biblical texts), and the references to it fall beneath that title; thus

Genesis
1.1-3   26
2.8   356
3.14-15   29

Exodus
22.18   122
25.7   321

A line of white space separates each work, as in the example above.

23.16	*Names of Other Ancient Texts.* The names of ancient texts are not spelled out in full in the case of Qumran and related texts (they appear as *1QM, 1QS, 4QFlor*, etc.; note the italics for the index headings, even though in the text of the book roman is used). Qumran texts are arranged by cave number, then alphabetically; CD and other texts without cave numbers follow, arranged simply alphabetically.

Tractates of the Mishnah, the Talmuds and the Tosefta have their names in italics (see further, §24.13). For Philo, the 'De' as the first word of the title is omitted (thus *Dec.*, not *De Decalogo*), and the names of the works are alphabetized according to the abbreviated form. Other ancient texts generally have as full a title as can reasonably be supplied.

23.17	*Order of References.* In indexes of references, the larger block of text precedes the smaller. Thus the correct order is:

> *Genesis*
> 1–3
> 1–2
> 1
> 1.1–3.6
> 1.1–3.5
> 1.1-4
> 1.1-3
> 1.1

23.18	*Apocrypha.* The books of the Apocrypha should usually come between the Old Testament and the New Testament (references should be arranged in the traditional order of the books; see §24.2). If there are only a few references to the Apocrypha, they are listed at the end of the Old Testament, without a special heading. Only if they run to more than 20 or 30 references are they separated off with a cross-heading of their own, APOCRYPHA.

23.19	*Pseudepigrapha.* Pseudepigrapha should be headed with the word PSEUDEPIGRAPHA (whether as a cross-heading or as a column will depend on the number of references); the books should be arranged alphabetically (for a list of the Pseudepigrapha, see §24.5). The headings in the columns should have the names spelled out in full (as with biblical books).

23.20 *Early Christian Authors*. Early Christian Authors are sometimes combined with the Pseudepigrapha into one alphabetical index (since the two frequently overlap), as are the Nag Hammadi tractates (rarely will a separate index of Nag Hammadi tractates be necessary). The decision is made on the basis of the number of texts represented in each category and the nature of the volume.

23.21 *Mishnah*. Mishnah references are always of the form *Ber.* 2.1; *Sanh.* 12.2 (i.e. abbreviated tractate name, chapter and verse). So too are references to the Tosefta. If it is necessary in the text to distinguish between Mishnah and Tosefta references, the appropriate forms used are: *m. Ber.* 2.1, *t. Ber.* 2.1 (but in a context dealing only with the Mishnah, the notation *m.* may be omitted). In the headings in the index, the abbreviated form of the Mishnah tractate name is to be used, e.g. *Ber.*, *Sukk.* The full list of tractate names appears in §24.13.

23.22 *Talmud*. Talmud references are always of the form *Ber.* 12a; *Sanh.* 37b (referring to the recto and verso of the page of the standard edition). It is to be assumed that references are to the Babylonian Talmud unless otherwise indicated (but in a passage dealing only with the Palestinian Talmud the prefixed notation *y.* may be omitted).

23.23 Arrange Talmudic references thus:

> Babylonian [abbreviated in the text by *b.*]
> Palestinian (also called Jerusalem) [abbreviated in the text
> by *y.* (for Yerushalmi, Jerusalemite)]

It is not necessary to repeat the distinction of Babylonian (*b.*) or Palestinian (*y.*) Talmud with each entry in the index, if the column heading makes the distinction clear.

23.24 In the headings in the index, the abbreviated form is used of the Talmud tractate, e.g. *Ber.*, *Sukk.* The entries are alphabetized according to the abbreviated forms. The full list of Talmud tractates appears in §24.13.

23.25   *Tosefta.* Tosefta references have the form *Ber.* 2.1; *Sanh.* 12.2. If it is necessary in the text to distinguish between Mishnah and Tosefta references, the appropriate forms are: *m. Ber.* 2.1, *t. Ber.* 2.1. But in a context dealing only with the Tosefta, the notation *t.* may be omitted. Entries are alphabetized according to the abbreviated forms.

23.26   *Midrashim.* There are two main groups of Midrashim, the Midrash Rabbah (Great Midrash), and various other minor midrashim. Arrange references in this order:

> Midrash Rabbah (arranged by order of biblical book)
> Other Midrashim (arranged alphabetically)

If there are only a few references to the Midrashim, they can all be arranged alphabetically.

23.27   *Midrash Rabbah.* The books of the Midrash Rabbah are (with SAP standard abbreviations in square brackets):

> *Genesis Rabbah (= Bereshith Rabbah) [Gen. R.]*
> *Exodus Rabbah (= Shemoth Rabbah) [Exod. R.]*
> *Leviticus Rabbah (= Vayyiqra Rabbah) [Lev. R.]*
> *Numbers Rabbah (= Bemidbar Rabbah) [Num. R.]*
> *Deuteronomy Rabbah (= Debarim Rabbah) [Deut. R.]*
> *Canticles Rabbah (= Shir Rabbah) [Cant. R.]*
> *Ruth Rabbah [Ruth R.]*
> *Lamentations Rabbah (= Ekah Rabbah) [Lam. R.]*
> *Qoheleth Rabbah [Qoh. R.]*
> *Esther Rabbah [Esth. R.]*

23.28   *Other Midrashim.* The other midrashim are as follows (arranged alphabetically, with SAP standard abbreviations in square brackets):

> *Chronicle of Moses*
> *Chronicle of Jerahmeel*
> *Mekilta [midrash on Exodus] [Mek.]*
> *Mekilta de Rabbi Simeon b. Johai [midrash on Exodus]*
>   *[Mek. SbY]*
> *Midrash haGadol*
> *Midrash on Proverbs [Midr. Prov.]*
> *Midrash on Samuel [Midr. Sam.]*
> *Midrash on Psalms (= Midrash Tehillim) [Midr. Pss.]*

Pesiqta (= *Pesiqta deRab Kahana*; references to edition of
  Mandelbaum [preferably] or S. Buber; form of refer-
  ence: *Pes. K.* 12a) [*Pes. K.*]
Pesiqta Rabbati (ed. Friedmann; trans. by W.G. Braude;
  form of reference: *Pes. R.* 14a) [*Pes. R.*]
Pirqe deRabbi Eliezer [*PRE*]
Sefer haYashar
Sifra (midrash on Leviticus)
Sifre (midrash on Numbers, Deuteronomy)
Sifre Zuta (another midrash on Numbers)
Tanḥuma (= Yelammedenu) (form of reference: *Tanḥ.* 12a
  or *Tanḥ.* on Gen. 1.1 or *Tanḥ.* B. [ref. to Buber's
  edition, 1885]) [*Tanḥ.*]

23.29 *Other Ancient Jewish Works.* Other ancient Jewish
works should be listed alphabetically, in one group, unless there
are very many references to one work, e.g. the Zohar. Mediaeval writers, such as Rashi, Maimonides, etc., should be
indexed in the author index. For other ancient Jewish works, see
§24.14.

23.30 *Philo.* Philo's works are arranged alphabetically, using
Latin titles (without the initial *De*), and in abbreviated form (see
the list of Philo's works in §24.7). Note that some works of Philo
have more than one 'book' in them, which is to be included in a
proper citation of the text according to our style of separating
books and chapters by full stops: e.g. *Leg. All.* 3.1.4. Thus some
references to Philo's works may have a larger number of divisions than do others. *Leg. All.* has three 'books', *Somn.* has two
and *Spec. Leg.* has four.

23.31 *Josephus.* The works of Josephus (listed in §24.8) are
arranged alphabetically: *Ant., Apion, Life, War.* Note that
Josephus's works are referred to by their English titles.

C. Reference

In this Section of the Manual, several kinds of tables of reference have been assembled, especially of standardized forms of reference and abbreviations for works commonly cited in biblical studies.

24. ABBREVIATIONS

24.1 For general rules about abbreviations, see §17.

24.2 *Biblical Books in Canonical Order*

Old Testament

Gen.	2 Kgs (LXX	Ezek.
Exod.	4 Kgdms)	Dan.
Lev.	1 Chron.	Hos.
Num.	2 Chron.	Joel
Deut.	Ezra	Amos
Josh.	Neh.	Obad.
Judg.	Est.	Jon.
Ruth	Job	Mic.
1 Sam. (LXX	Ps. (pl. Pss.)	Nah.
1 Kgdms)	Prov.	Hab.
2 Sam. (LXX	Eccl. (or Qoh.)	Zeph.
2 Kgdms)	Song (or Cant.)	Hag.
1 Kgs (LXX	Isa.	Zech.
3 Kgdms)	Jer.	Mal.
	Lam.	

Apocrypha or Deutero-Canonical books

1 Esd.	Add. Est.	Dan. 3.26-45
2 Esd. [chs. 3–14	Wis.	is Prayer of
are 4 *Ezra* in	Sir. (*or* Ecclus)	Azariah]
the Pseude-	Bar.	Bel
pigrapha]	Ep. Jer.	Pr. Man.
Tob.	Song 3 Childr.	1 Macc.
Jdt.	[Dan. 3.24-90;	2 Macc.

New Testament

Mt.	Lk.	Acts
Mk	Jn	Rom.

1 Cor.	2 Thess.	1 Pet.
2 Cor.	1 Tim.	2 Pet.
Gal.	2 Tim.	1 Jn
Eph.	Tit.	2 Jn
Phil.	Phlm.	3 Jn
Col.	Heb.	Jude
1 Thess.	Jas	Rev.

24.3 *Biblical Books in Alphabetical Order*

1 Chron.	Dan.	Lev.
2 Chron.	Deut.	Lk.
1 Cor.	Eccl. (or Qoh.)	Mal.
2 Cor.	Ecclus (or Sir.)	Mic.
1 Esd.	Ep. Jer.	Mk
2 Esd.	Eph.	Mt.
1 Jn	Est.	Nah.
2 Jn	Exod.	Neh.
3 Jn	Ezek.	Num.
1 Kgs	Ezra	Obad.
2 Kgs	Gal.	Phil.
1 Macc.	Gen.	Phlm.
2 Macc.	Hab.	Pr. Man.
1 Pet.	Hag.	Prov.
2 Pet.	Heb.	Ps. (pl. Pss.)
1 Sam.	Hos.	Qoh. (or Eccl.)
2 Sam.	Isa.	Rev.
1 Thess.	Jas	Rom.
2 Thess.	Jdt.	Ruth
1 Tim.	Jer.	Sir. (*or* Ecclus)
2 Tim.	Jn	Song (or Cant.)
Acts	Job	Song 3 Childr.
Add. Est.	Joel	Tit.
Amos	Jon.	Tob.
Bar.	Josh.	Wis.
Bel	Jude	Zech.
Cant. (or Song)	Judg.	Zeph.
Col.	Lam.	

24.4. *Pseudepigrapha*

The following works known as the Pseudepigrapha are those included in the current standard English translation, James H. Charlesworth (ed.), *The Old Testament Pseudepigrapha* (2 vols.; London: Darton, Longman & Todd, 1983, 1985).

24.5 Though some of the names listed below are those of the authors or presumed authors of texts, it is conventional to regard the name of the author as the name of the work, and so to set both the abbreviation and the full title in italics.

1 En.	*1 (Ethiopic) Enoch*
2 En.	*2 (Slavonic) Enoch*
3 En.	*3 (Hebrew) Enoch*
2 Bar.	*2 (Syriac) Baruch [= Apocalypse of Baruch]*
3 Bar.	*3 (Greek) Baruch*
4 Bar.	*4 Baruch*
3 Macc.	*3 Maccabees*
4 Macc.	*4 Maccabees*
4 Ezra	*4 Ezra [= 2 Esd. 3–14]*
Ahiqar	*Ahiqar*
Apoc. Abr.	*Apocalypse of Abraham*
Apoc. Adam	*Apocalypse of Adam*
Apoc. Dan.	*Apocalypse of Daniel*
Apoc. Elij.	*Apocalypse of Elijah*
Apoc. Sedr.	*Apocalypse of Sedrach*
Apoc. Zeph.	*Apocalypse of Zephaniah*
Apocr. Ezek.	*Apocryphon of Ezekiel*
Arist. Exeg.	*Aristeas the Exegete*
Aristob.	*Aristobulus*
Art.	*Artapanus*
Cl. Mal.	*Cleodemus Malchus*
Dem.	*Demetrius (the Chronographer)*
El. Mod.	*Eldad and Modad*
Ep. Arist.	*Letter of Aristeas*
Eupol.	*Eupolemus*
Ezek. Trag.	*Ezekiel the Tragedian*
Fr. Ps.-Gk Poets	*Fragments of Pseudo-Greek Poets*
Gk. Apoc. Ezra	*Greek Apocalypse of Ezra*
Hell. Syn. Pr.	*Hellenistic Synagogal Prayers*
Hist. Jos.	*History of Joseph*
Hist. Rech.	*History of the Rechabites*
Jan. Jam.	*Jannes and Jambres*
Jos. Asen.	*Joseph and Asenath (or, Aseneth)*
Jub.	*Jubilees*
Lad. Jac.	*Ladder of Jacob*
LAE	*Life of Adam and Eve*
Liv. Proph.	*Lives of the Prophets*
Mart. Isa.	*Martyrdom of Isaiah*
Odes	*Odes of Solomon*
Orph.	*Orphica*

Ph. E. Poet	*Philo the Epic Poet*
Pr. Jac.	*Prayer of Jacob*
Pr. Jos.	*Prayer of Joseph*
Pr. Man.	*Prayer of Manasseh*
Ps.-Eupol.	*Pseudo-Eupolemus*
Ps.-Hec.	*Pseudo-Hecataeus*
Ps.-Philo	*Pseudo-Philo*
Ps.-Phoc.	*Pseudo-Phocylides*
Pss. Dav.	*More Psalms of David*
Pss. Sol.	*Psalms of Solomon*
Ques. Ezra	*Questions of Ezra*
Rev. Ezra	*Revelation of Ezra*
Sib. Or.	*Sibylline Oracles*
Syr. Men.	*Syriac Menander*
T. Adam	*Testament of Adam*
T. Hez.	*Testament of Hezekiah*
T. Job	*Testament of Job*
T. Mos.	*Testament of Moses*
T. Sol.	*Testament of Solomon*
Test. III Patr.	*Testaments of the Three Patriarchs*
T. Abr.	*Testament of Abraham*
T. Isaac	*Testament of Isaac*
T. Jac.	*Testament of Jacob*
Test. XII Patr.	*Testaments of the Twelve Patriarchs*
T. Ash.	*Testament of Asher*
T. Benj.	*Testament of Benjamin*
T. Dan	*Testament of Dan*
T. Gad	*Testament of Gad*
T. Iss.	*Testament of Issachar*
T. Jos.	*Testament of Joseph*
T. Jud.	*Testament of Judah*
T. Levi	*Testament of Levi*
T. Naph.	*Testament of Naphtali*
T. Reub.	*Testament of Reuben*
T. Sim.	*Testament of Simeon*
T. Zeb.	*Testament of Zebulun*
Theod.	*Theodotus*
Tr. Shem	*Treatise of Shem*
Vis. Ezra	*Vision of Ezra*

24.6 *Other Early Jewish and Christian Literature*

1–2 Clem.	*1–2 Clement*
5 Apoc. Syr. Pss.	*Five Apocryphal Syriac Psalms*
5 Macc.	*5 Maccabees*

Acts Pil.	*Acts of Pilate*
Anon. Sam.	*An Anonymous Samaritan Text*
Apoc. Mos.	*Apocalypse of Moses*
Apoc. Pet.	*Apocalypse of Peter*
Apoc. Zos.	*Apocalypse of Zosimus*
Asc. Isa.	*Ascension of Isaiah*
Ass. Mos.	*Assumption of Moses*
Barn.	*Barnabas*
Bk Noah	*Book of Noah*
Cav. Tr.	*Cave of Treasures*
Did.	*Didache*
Diogn.	*Diognetus*
Fr. Hist. Wk.	*Fragments of Historical Works*
Fr. Poet. Wk.	*Fragments of Poetical Works*
Gos. Eb.	*Gospel of the Ebionites*
Gos. Eg.	*Gospel of the Egyptians*
Gos. Heb.	*Gospel of the Hebrews*
Gos. Naass.	*Gospel of the Naassenes*
Gos. Pet.	*Gospel of Peter*
Gos. Thom.	*Gospel of Thomas*
Heb. Apoc. Elij.	*Hebrew Apocalypse of Elijah*
Hec. Ab.	*Hecataeus of Abdera*
Hermas, *Man.*	Hermas, *Mandate*
Hermas, *Sim.*	Hermas, *Similitude*
Hermas, *Vis.*	Hermas, *Vision*
Ignatius, *Eph.*	Ignatius, *Letter to the Ephesians*
Ignatius, *Magn.*	Ignatius, *Letter to the Magnesians*
Ignatius, *Phld.*	Ignatius, *Letter to the Philadelphians*
Ignatius, *Pol.*	Ignatius, *Letter to Polycarp*
Ignatius, *Rom.*	Ignatius, *Letter to the Romans*
Ignatius, *Smyrn.*	Ignatius, *Letter to the Smyrnaeans*
Ignatius, *Trall.*	Ignatius, *Letter to the Trallians*
LAB	*Liber Antiquitatum Biblicarum*
Lost Tr.	*The Lost Tribes*
Mart. Pol.	*Martyrdom of Polycarp*
Par. Jer.	*Paraleipomena Jeremiou*
Polycarp, *Phil.*	Polycarp, *Philippians*
Pr. Mos.	*Prayer of Moses*
Prot. Jas.	*Protevangelium of James*
Ps.-Men.	*Pseudo-Menander*
Ps.-Orph.	*Pseudo-Orpheus*
Thal.	*Thallus*
Vis. Isa.	*Vision of Isaiah*

24.7 *Philo*

Abr.	*De Abrahamo*
Aet. Mund.	*De aeternitate mundi*
Agr.	*De agricultura*
Cher.	*De cherubim*
Conf. Ling.	*De confusione linguarum*
Congr.	*De congressu eruditionis gratia*
Dec.	*De decalogo*
Det. Pot. Ins.	*Quod deterius potiori insidiari soleat*
Deus Imm.	*Quod Deus sit immutabilis*
Ebr.	*De ebrietate*
Exsecr.	*De exsecrationibus*
Flacc.	*Against Flaccus,* or *In Flaccum,* or *Contra Flaccum*
Fug.	*De fuga et inventione*
Gig.	*De gigantibus*
Jos.	*De Josepho*
Leg. All.	*Legum allegoriae*
Leg. Gai.	*Legatio ad Gaium*
Migr. Abr.	*De migratione Abrahami*
Mut. Nom.	*De mutatione nominum*
Omn. Prob. Lib.	*Quod omnis probus liber sit*
Op. Mund.	*De opificio mundi*
Plant.	*De plantatione*
Poster. C.	*De posteritate Caini*
Praem. Poen.	*De praemiis et poenis*
Quaest. in Gen.	*Quaestiones in Genesin*
Quaest. in Exod.	*Quaestiones in Exodum*
Rer. Div. Her.	*Quis rerum divinarum heres sit*
Sacr.	*De sacrificiis Abelis et Caini*
Sobr.	*De sobrietate*
Somn.	*De somniis*
Spec. Leg.	*De specialibus legibus*
Virt.	*De virtutibus*
Vit. Cont.	*De vita contemplativa*
Vit. Mos.	*De vita Mosis*

24.8 *Josephus*

Ant.	*Antiquities of the Jews*
Apion	*Against Apion,* or *Contra Apionem*
Life	*Life of Josephus,* or *Vita Josephi*
War	*The Jewish War,* or *De Bello Judaico*

24.9 *Dead Sea Scrolls*

The nomenclature of the Dead Sea Scrolls and related texts is a complicated matter. All the manuscripts have a reference number, typically in the form 4Q186, the number before the Q indicating the cave in which the text in question was discovered, and the number after being the number of the manuscript from that cave. But in many cases the manuscripts are usually referred to by an abbreviation ('siglum') that gives some clue to their contents; thus 4Q186, which contains horoscopes, is often referred to as 4QCrypt (occasionally, more than one siglum is in current use). Below is a complete list of Dead Sea Scrolls and related texts, in the order of the reference numbers, and showing the siglum and the conventional name (in upper and lower case and in italic) or (briefly) the contents (in lower case and in roman).

24.10   Qumran reference numbers and sigla are set in roman type (thus 4Q186, 4QCrypt). The full names by which they are conventionally known, such as *Manual of Discipline, Wiles of the Wicked Woman*, are set in italic.

24.11   The list below is reproduced from David J.A. Clines (ed.), *The Dictionary of Classical Hebrew*. III. *Zayin–Tet* (Sheffield: Sheffield Academic Press, 1996), pp. 12-23. In those pages, in addition to the information given here, the primary publication of the text is also cited, and the page reference in the translation by Florentino García Martínez, *The Dead Sea Scrolls Translated: The Qumran Texts in English* (trans. Wilfred G.E. Watson; Leiden: E.J. Brill, 1994).

Number	*Siglum*	*Name / Description*
Cave 1		
	1QH	*Hymns / Hodayot*
	1QM	*War Scroll*
	1QpHab	*Habakkuk Pesher*
	1QS	*Community Rule / Manual of Discipline*
1Q14	1QpMic	*Micah Pesher*
1Q15	1QpZeph	*Zephaniah Pesher*
1Q16	1QpPs	*Psalms Pesher*
1Q17	1QJub^a	*Jubilees*

1Q18	1QJub^b	*Jubilees*

1Q18	1QJub^b	*Jubilees*
1Q19	1QNoah	*Noah*
1Q19b	1QNoah	*Noah*
1Q22	1QDM	*Dibre Mosheh / Words of Moses*
1Q25		prophecy
1Q26		sapiential
1Q27	1QMyst	prophecy
1Q28a	1QSa	*Community Rule*
1Q28b	1QSb	*Community Rule*
1Q29		*Three Tongues of Fire*
1Q30		liturgical
1Q31		liturgical
1Q33	1QM	*War Scroll*
1Q34	1QLitPr	*Festival Prayers*
1Q35	1QH^b	*Hymns/Hodayoth*
1Q36		hymns
1Q37–40		hymns
1Q41–62		unidentified
1Q69		unidentified

Cave 2

2Q19	2QJub^a	*Jubilees*
2Q20	2QJub^b	*Jubilees*
2Q21	2QapMoses	*Apocryphon of Moses*
2Q22	2QapDavid	*Apocryphon of David*
2Q23	2QapProph	prophecy
2Q25		halakhah
2Q27–33		unidentified

Cave 3

3Q4	3QpIsa	*Isaiah Pesher*
3Q5	3QJub	*Jubilees*
3Q6	3QHymn	hymnic
3Q7	3QTJud	*Testament of Judah*
3Q8		*Angel of Peace*
3Q9		sectarian
3Q10-11		unidentified
3Q15	3QTr	*Copper Scroll*

Cave 4

4Q158	4QBibPar	*Biblical Paraphrase*
4Q159	4QOrd^a	*Ordinances*
4Q160	4QVisSam	*Visions of Samuel*

4Q161	4QpIsa^a	*Isaiah Pesher*
4Q162	4QpIsa^b	*Isaiah Pesher*
4Q163	4QpIsa^c	*Isaiah Pesher*
4Q164	4QpIsa^d	*Isaiah Pesher*
4Q165	4QpIsa^e	*Isaiah Pesher*
4Q166	4QpHos^a	*Hosea Pesher*
4Q167	4QpHos^b	*Hosea Pesher*
4Q168	4QpMic	*Micah Pesher*
4Q169	4QpNah	*Nahum Pesher*
4Q170	4QpZeph	*Zephaniah Pesher*
4Q171	4QpPs^a	*Psalms Pesher*
4Q172	4QpUnid	unidentified pesher
4Q173	4QpPs^b	*Psalms Pesher*
4Q174	4QMidrEschat^a	eschatological
4Q175	4QTestim	*Testimonia*
4Q176	4QTanḥ	*Consolations*
4Q176.19-21	4QJub^f	*Jubilees*
4Q177	4QMidrEschat^b	eschatological
4Q178		unidentified
4Q179	4QapLam^a	*Lamentation on Jerusalem*
4Q180	4QAges	*Pesher on the Periods*
4Q181		*Ages of Creation*
4Q182	4QCat	*Catena*
4Q183		historical
4Q184	4QWiles	*Wiles of the Wicked Woman*
4Q185		*Eulogy on Wisdom*
4Q186	4QCrypt	horoscopes
4Q200	4QTob	*Tobit*
4Q215	4QTNaph	*Testament of Naphtali*
4Q216	4QJub^a	*Jubilees*^a
4Q217	4QJub^b	*Jubilees*^b
4Q218	4QJub^c	*Jubilees*^c
4Q219	4QJub^d	*Jubilees*^d
4Q220	4QJub^e	*Jubilees*^e
4Q221	4QJub^f	*Jubilees*^f
4Q222	4QJub^g	*Jubilees*^g
4Q223–224	4QJub^h	*Jubilees*^h
4Q225	4QpsJub^a	
4Q226	4QpsJub^b	
4Q227	4QpsJub^c	*Pseudo-Jubilees*
4Q228		work citing Jubilees
4Q229		pseudepigraphon (Mishnaic)
4Q230		*Catalogue of Spirits*^a

4Q231		*Catalogue of Spirits*b
4Q232		*New Jerusalem (?)*
4Q233		place names
4Q234		exercise on Genesis 27
4Q237		psalter
4Q239		pesher on the true Israel
4Q240		commentary on Canticles (?)
4Q241		fragments citing Lamentations
4Q247		pesher on Apocalypse of Weeks
4Q248		*Acts of a Greek King*
4Q249	4QMSM	*Midrash Sepher Mosheh*
4Q250		text on verso of MSM
4Q251		*Halakhah/A Pleasing Fragrance*
4Q252	4QpGena	*Patriarchal Blessings /*
		Genesis Florilegium
4Q253	4QpGenb	*Patriarchal Blessings /*
		commentary on Malachi?
4Q254	4QpGenc	*Patriarchal Blessings*
4Q254a		*Genesis Florilegium*
4Q255	4QSa	*Community Rule*
4Q256	4QSb	*Community Rule* (previously 4QS)
4Q257	4QSc	*Community Rule*
4Q258	4QSd	*Community Rule* (previously 4QS)
4Q259	4QSe	*Community Rule*
4Q260	4QSf	*Community Rule*
4Q261	4QSg	*Community Rule*
4Q262	4QSh	*Community Rule*
4Q263	4QSi	*Community Rule*
4Q264	4QSj	*Community Rule*
4Q265	4QSD	*Community Rule +*
		Damascus Document
4Q266	4QDa	*Damascus Document* a
4Q267	4QDb	*Damascus Document*b
4Q268	4QDc	*Damascus Document*c
4Q269	4QDd	*Damascus Document*d
4Q270	4QDe	*Damascus Document*e
4Q271	4QDf	*Damascus Document*f
4Q272	4QDg	*Damascus Document*g
4Q273	4QDh	*Damascus Document*h
4Q274	4QTohA	*Purities*
4Q275	4QTohB	*Purities*
4Q276	4QTohBa	*Laws of the Red Heifer*
4Q277	4QTohBb	*Laws of the Red Heifer*

4Q278	4QTohC?	
4Q279	4QTohD^a?	*Laws*
4Q280	4QTohD	*Curses against Melkiresha*
4Q281–282	4QTohE^a?	
4Q283	4QTohF?	
4Q284	4QNid	*Rule of the Menstruants*
4Q284a		*Leqet*
4Q285		*Destruction of the Kittim /*
		Messianic Leader
4Q286	4QBer^a	*The Chariots of Glory*
4Q287	4QBer^b	*The Chariots of Glory*
4Q288	4QBer^c	
4Q289	4QBer^d	
4Q290	4QBer^e	
4Q291–293		prayers
4Q294–297		rules and prayers
4Q298		*Admonitions to the Sons of Dawn*
4Q299	4QMyst^a	= 1Q27
4Q300	4QMyst^b	= 1Q27
4Q301	4QMyst^c	= 1Q27
4Q302		*Praise of God*
4Q302a		*Parable of the Tree*
4Q303		*Meditation on Creation A*^a
4Q304		*Meditation on Creation A*^b
4Q305		*Meditation on Creation B*
4Q306		*Men of People who Err*
4Q307		sapiential
4Q308		sapiential
4Q311		unidentified
4Q312		Hebrew text in cursive Phoenician
4Q313		unidentified cryptic script
4Q316		unidentified
4Q317		*Phases of Moon* (cryptic script)
4Q319	4QOtot	*Heavenly Concordances*
4Q320	4QMish A	*Priestly Courses II*
4Q321	4QMish B^a	*Priestly Courses I*
4Q321a	4QMish B^b	*Priestly Courses I*
4Q322	4QMish C^a	*Priestly Courses III*
4Q323	4QMish C^b	*Priestly Courses III*
4Q324	4QMish C^c	*Priestly Courses III*
4Q324a	4QMish C^d	*Priestly Courses III*
4Q324b	4QMish C^e	*Priestly Courses III*

4Q324c	4QMish C^f	
4Q325	4QMish D	*Priestly Courses IV*
4Q326	4QMish E^a	
4Q327	4QMish E^b	
4Q328	4QMish F^a	
4Q329	4QMish F^b	
4Q329a	4QMish G	
4Q330	4QMish H	
4Q331		*Historical Work*^{a}
4Q332		*Historical Work*^{b}
4Q333		*Historical Work*^{c}
4Q334	4QOrdo	*Ordo*
4Q335–336		astronomical
4Q337		calendar
4Q338		genealogical
4Q339		list of false prophets
4Q340		list of Nethinim
4Q341		list of proper names
4Q344		debt acknowledgment
4Q348		act regarding ownership
4Q349		sale of property
4Q356		account of money
4Q360		exercise / *Therapeia*
4Q362-63, 363a		cryptic script
4Q364	4QPentPar^a	*Pentateuchal Paraphrase*
4Q365	4QPentPar^b	*Pentateuchal Paraphrase*
4Q365a		*Temple Scroll?*
4Q366	4QPentPar^c	*Pentateuchal Paraphrase*
4Q367	4QPentPar^d	*Pentateuchal Paraphrase*
4Q368		*Pentateuch Apocryphon*
4Q369		*Prayer of Enosh?*
4Q370		*Flood Apocryphon*
4Q371	4QApocJos^a	*Joseph Apocryphon*
4Q372	4QApocJos^b	*Joseph Apocryphon*
4Q373	4QApocJos^c	*Joseph Apocryphon*
4Q374	4QApocMos A	*Moses Apocryphon A*
4Q375	4QApocMos B	*Moses Apocryphon B*
4Q376		*Three Tongues of Fire*
4Q377	4QApocMos C	*Moses Apocryphon C*
4Q378	4QPsJos^a	*Psalms of Joshua*
4Q379	4QPsJos^b	*Psalms of Joshua*
4Q380	4QapPs^a	*Non-Canonical Psalms A*
4Q381	4QapPs^b	*Non-Canonical Psalms B*

4Q382		*Kings Paraphrase*
4Q383	4QApocJer A	*Jeremiah Apocryphon A*
4Q384	4QApocJer B	*Jeremiah Apocryphon B*
4Q385	4QpsEzek^a	*Pseudo-Ezekiel*
4Q385a	4QpsMos^a	*Pseudo-Moses*
4Q385b	4QApocJer C	*Jeremiah Apocryphon C*
4Q386–389	4QpsEzek^b	*Second Ezekiel*, etc.
4Q390	4QpsMos^e	*Pseudo-Moses Apocalypse / Angels of Mastemoth*
4Q391	4QpsEzek^g	*Pseudo-Ezekiel*
4Q392-93		liturgical
4Q394–99	4QMMT	*Halakah / Letter on Works*
4Q400	4QShirShabb^a	*Songs of the Sabbath Sacrifice*
4Q401	4QShirShabb^b	*Songs of the Sabbath Sacrifice*
4Q402	4QShirShabb^c	*Songs of the Sabbath Sacrifice*
4Q403	4QShirShabb^d	*Songs of the Sabbath Sacrifice*
4Q404	4QShirShabb^e	*Songs of the Sabbath Sacrifice*
4Q405	4QShirShabb^f	*Songs of the Sabbath Sacrifice*
4Q406	4QShirShabb^g	*Songs of the Sabbath Sacrifice*
4Q407	4QShirShabb^h	*Songs of the Sabbath Sacrifice*
4Q408		sapiential
4Q409		liturgical
4Q410		sapiential
4Q411		sapiential
4Q412		sapiential
4Q413		sapiential
4Q414		*Baptismal Hymn*
4Q415		*Sapiential Work A^d*
4Q416		*Sapiential Work A^b / The Children of Salvation*
4Q417		*Sapiential Work A^c*
4Q418		*Sapiential Work A^a / The Children of Salvation*
4Q419		*Sapiential Work B*
4Q420		*Ways of Righteousness^a*
4Q421		*Ways of Righteousness^b*
4Q422		*Treatise on Genesis and Exodus*
4Q423		*Sapiential Work A^e*
4Q423a		*Sapiential Work E*
4Q424		sapiential / *The Sons of Righteousness*
4Q425		*Sapiential Work C*
4Q426		sapiential

4Q427	4QHod^a	*Hymns*
4Q428	4QHod^b	*Hymns*
4Q429	4QHod^c	*Hymns*
4Q430	4QHod^d	*Hymns*
4Q431	4QHod^e	*Hymns*
4Q432	4QHod^f	*Hymns*
4Q433		hymnic
4Q434	4QBark^a	*Barki Naphshi^a*
4Q434a		*Grace after Meals*
4Q435	4QBark^b	*Barki Naphshi^b*
4Q436	4QBark^c	*Barki Naphshi^c*
4Q437	4QBark^d	*Barki Naphshi^d*
4Q438	4QBark^e	*Barki Naphshi^e*
4Q439		similar to Barki Naphshi
4Q440		hymnic
4Q441–444		prayers
4Q445–447		poetic
4Q448		*Paean for King Jonathan*
		Apocryphal Psalms
4Q449–457		prayers
4Q458		*The Tree of Evil*
4Q459–460		pseudepigraphic
4Q461		narrative
4Q462		*Second Exodus /*
		The Era of Light is Coming
4Q463		sapiential
4Q464		*Exposition on the Patriarchs*
4Q464a-b, 465		unidentified
4Q466–469		apocryphon
4Q470		Zedekiah fragment
4Q471	4QM^h	*The Servants of Darkness*
4Q471a		polemical
4Q472		sapiential
4Q473		*The Two Ways*
4Q474–475		sapiential
4Q476		sapiential
4Q477		*Decrees of Sect / He Loved*
		His Bodily Emissions
4Q479–481a-f		unidentified
4Q482		*Jubilees?*
4Q483		*Jubilees?*
4Q484	4QTJud	*Testament of Judah*
4Q485	4QProph	prophetic or sapiential
4Q486	4QSap^a	sapiential

4Q487	4QSap^b	sapiential
4Q491	4QM^a	*War Scroll*
4Q492	4QM^b	*War Scroll*
4Q493	4QM^c	*War Scroll*
4Q494	4QM^d	*War Scroll*
4Q495	4QM^e	*War Scroll*
4Q496	4QM^f	*War Scroll*
4Q497	4QM$^{g(?)}$	*War Scroll*
4Q498	4QHymSap	hymnic or sapiential
4Q499	4QHymPr	hymnic or prayers
4Q500	4QBen	*Song of the Vineyard*
4Q501	4QapLam^b	*Lamentation*
4Q502	4QRitMar	*Ritual of Marriage*
4Q503	4QPrQuot	*Daily Prayers*
4Q504	4QDibHam^a	*Words of the Luminaries*
4Q505	4QDibHam^b	*Words of the Luminaries*
4Q506	4QDibHam^c	*Words of the Luminaries*
4Q507	4QPrFêtes^a	*Festival Prayers*
4Q508	4QPrFêtes^b	*Festival Prayers*
4Q509	4QPrFêtes^c	*Festival Prayers*
4Q510	4QShir^a	*Songs of the Sage*
4Q511	4QShir^b	*Songs of the Sage*
4Q512	4QRitPur	*Ritual of Purification*
4Q513	4QOrd^b	*Ordinances*
4Q514	4QOrd^c	*Ordinances*
4Q515–520		unidentified fragments
4Q521		*Messiah of Heaven and Earth*
4Q522		*Joshua Apocryphon*
4Q523		Hebrew fragment B
4Q524		halakic
4Q525		*Beatitudes /*
		The Demons of Death
4Q526		Hebrew fragment C
4Q527		Hebrew fragment D
4Q528		Hebrew fragment E
4QAcademyFr		*Academy Fragments*

Cave 5

5Q9		toponyms
5Q10	5QapMal	*Malachi Pesher?*
5Q11	5QS	*Community Rule*
5Q12	5QD	*Damascus Document*
5Q13	5QRègle	*Damascus Document + Rule*

| 5Q14 | | curses |
| 5Q16–25 | | unclassified |

Cave 6

6Q9	6QapSam/Kings	Samuel–Kings apocryphon
6Q10	6QProph	prophetic
6Q11	6QAllegory	*Song of the Vine*
6Q12	6QapProph	prophetic
6Q13	6QPriestProph	priestly prophecy
6Q15	6QD	*Damascus Document*
6Q16	6QBen	blessings
6Q17	6QCal	calendar
6Q18	6QHym	hymnic
6Q20	6QDeut(?)	Deuteronomy-related?
6Q21	6QfrProph	unidentified
6Q22		unidentified
6Q24–25		unidentified
6Q26		account or contract
6Q27–31		unclassified
6QX1–2		unclassified

Cave 8

| 8Q3 | 8QPhyl | phylactery |
| 8Q5 | 8QHymn | hymnic |

Cave 9

| 9Q | | unclassified |

Cave 10

| 10Q | | ostracon? |

Cave 11

11Q5	11QPs^a	
11Q11	11QapPs^a	*Apocryphal Psalms*
11Q12	11QJub	*Jubilees*
11Q13	11QMelch	*Melchizedek*
11Q14	11QBer	*Benedictions* (= 4Q285)
11Q15	11QHod^a	*Hymns*
11Q16	11QHod^b	*Hymns*
11Q17	11QShirShabb	*Songs of the Sabbath Sacrifice*
11Q19–20	11QT	*Temple Scroll*
11QT^b		*Temple Scroll*
11Q21–23		unidentified

Masada

MasShirShabb *Songs of the Sabbath Sacrifice*

Murabba'at

Mur 6		hymnic
Mur 7		contract
Mur 22		deed of sale of land
Mur 24		farming contracts
Mur 29		deed of sale
Mur 30		deed of sale
Mur 42	MurEpBeth-Mashiko	letter of administrators
Mur 43	MurEpBarC^a	letter of Shimon b. Kosibah
Mur 44	MurEpBarC^b	letter of Shimon b. Kosibah
Mur 45		letter
Mur 46	MurEpJonathan	
letter of Jonathan		
Mur 47		letter
Mur 48		letter

Naḥal Ḥever

5/6 ḤevBA 44	contract
5/6 ḤevBA fr. 1–2	contract
5/6 ḤevBA 45	contract
5/6 ḤevBA 45 fr. 1–2	
5/6 ḤevBA 46	contract
5/6 ḤevEp 1	letter
5/6 ḤevEp 5	letter
5/6 ḤevEp 12	letter
5/6 ḤevEp 12 fr.	letter

24.12 *Rabbinic Writings*

For further details about these texts, see the rules for Indexes, §23.

24.13 *Tractates of the Mishnah and Talmud*

The Mishnah is a collection of legal material, in Hebrew (Mishnaic Hebrew) from the second century CE. It is arranged in six Orders (which are rarely referred to in citations), each of which contains several tractates. The Talmud is a sentence by sentence elaboration of the Mishnah. The expansion is in Aramaic and is known as Gemara (completion). Mishnah and Gemara together constitute Talmud. The Talmud is arranged in the same order, with the same tractates, as the Mishnah. There are two Talmuds, the Babylonian (also known as Bavli) and the Jerusalem (also known as Yerushalmi).

Ab.	*Abot*
'Abod. Zar.	*'Abodah Zarah*
'Arak.	*'Arakin*
B. Bat.	*Baba Batra*
Bek.	*Bekorot*
Ber.	*Berakot*
Beṣ.	*Beṣah (= Yom Ṭob)*
Bikk.	*Bikkurim*
B. Meṣ.	*Baba Meṣi'a*
B. Qam.	*Baba Qamma*
Dem.	*Demai*
'Ed.	*'Eduyyot*
'Erub.	*'Erubin*
Giṭ.	*Giṭṭin*
Ḥag.	*Ḥagigah*
Ḥal.	*Ḥallah*
Hor.	*Horayot*
Ḥul.	*Ḥullin*
Kel.	*Kelim*
Ker.	*Keritot*
Ket.	*Ketubot*
Kil.	*Kilaim*
Kin.	*Kinnim*
Ma'as.	*Ma'aserot*
Mak.	*Makkot*
Makš.	*Makširin (= Mašqin)*
Meg.	*Megillah*
Me'il.	*Me'ilah*
Men.	*Menaḥot*
Mid.	*Middot*
Miq.	*Miqwa'ot*
M. Qaṭ.	*Mo'ed Qaṭan*
Ma'as. Š.	*Ma'aser Šeni*
Našim	*Našim*
Naz.	*Nazir*
Ned.	*Nedarim*
Neg.	*Nega'im*
Nez.	*Neziqin*
Nid.	*Niddah*
Ohol.	*Oholot*
'Or.	*'Orlah*
Par.	*Parah*

Pe'ah	Pe'ah
Pes.	Pesaḥim
Qid.	Qiddušin
Qinnim	Qinnim
Qod.	Qodašin
Roš Haš.	Roš haš-Šanah
Šab.	Šabbat
Sanh.	Sanhedrin
Šeb.	Šebi'it
Šebu.	Šebu'ot
Šeq.	Šeqalim
Soṭ.	Soṭah
Suk.	Sukkah
Ta'an.	Ta'anit
Tam.	Tamid
Ṭeb. Y.	Ṭebul Yom
Tem.	Temurah
Ter.	Terumot
Ṭoh.	Ṭohorot
'Uq.	'Uqṣin
Yad.	Yadaim
Yeb.	Yebamot
Yom.	Yoma (= Kippurim)
Zab.	Zabim
Zeb.	Zebaḥi m
Zer.	Zera'im

24.14   Further Rabbinic Abbreviations

Ag. Ber.	Aggadat Berešit
ARN	Abot deRabbi Nathan
b.	Babylonian Talmud
Bar.	Baraita
Bem. R.	Bemidbar Midrash (Midrash Rabbah on Numbers) [preferably Num. R.]
Ber. R.	Bereshith Midrash (Midrash Rabbah on Genesis) [preferably Gen. R.]
Cant. R.	Canticles Rabbah
Deb. R.	Debarim Midrash (Midrash Rabbah on Deuteronomy) [preferably Deut. R.]
Der. Er. Rab.	Derek Ereṣ Rabba
Der. Er. Zuṭ.	Derek Ereṣ Zuṭa
Deut. R.	Deuteronomy Rabbah
Eccl. R.	Ecclesiastes Rabbah
Est. R.	Esther Midrash (Midrash Rabbah on Esther)

Exod. R.	*Exodus Rabbah*
Frag. Targ.	*Fragmentary Targum*
Gem.	*Gemara*
Kalla	*Kalla*
Lam. R.	*Lamentations Rabbah*
m.	*Mishnah*
M. ha-Midd.	*Mishnat ha-Middot*
Meg. Ta'an.	*Megillat Ta'anit*
Mek.	*Mekilta deRabbi Ishmael*
Mek. SbY.	*Mekilta deRabbi Simeon ben Yoḥai*
Midr. Prov.	*Midrash on Proverbs*
Midr. Ps.	*Midrash on Psalms*
Midr. Tan.	*Midrash Tanna'im*
Midr. Teh.	*Midrash Tehillim (Midrash on Psalms)*
Neof.	*Neofiti I (Targum)* [or *Targ. Neof.*]
Num. R.	*Numbers Rabbah*
Pes. K.	*Pesiqta deRab Kahana* (usually cited from Mandelbaum's edition)
Pes. R.	*Pesiqta Rabbati*
PRE	*Pirke deRabbi Eliezer*
Pal. Targ.	*Palestinian Targum*
Qoh. R.	*Qohelet Midrash (Midrash Rabbah on Ecclesiastes)*
R.	*Rabbah*
Ruth R.	*Ruth Rabbah*
S. 'Ol. R.	*Seder 'Olam Rabbah*
Sam. Targ.	*Samaritan Targum*
Ṣem.	*Ṣemaḥot*
Shem. R.	*Shemoth Midrash (Midrash Rabbah on Exodus)* [preferably *Exod. R.*]
Shir. R.	*Shir hash-Shirim Midrash (Midrash Rabbah on Song of Songs)* [preferably *Cant. R.*]
Sifra	*Sifra* (= Midrash on Leviticus)
Sifre	*Sifre* (= Midrash on Numbers and Deuteronomy)
Sop.	*Soperim*
T. d. Eliyy.	*Tanna debe Eliyyahu (= Seder Eliyyahu Rabba)*
Tanḥ.	*Tanḥuma*
t.	*Tosefta*
Targ. Esth. I, II	*First or Second Targum of Esther*
Targ. Isa.	*Targum of Isaiah*
Targ. Ket.	*Targum of the Writings*
Targ. Neb.	*Targum of the Prophets*
Targ. Neof.	*Targum Neofiti I* [or *Neof.*]
Targ. Onq.	*Targum Onqelos*

Targ. Ps.-J.	*Targum Pseudo-Jonathan*
Vay. R.	*Vayyiqra Midrash (Midrash Rabbah on Leviticus)* [preferably *Lev. R.*]
y.	*Yerushalmi (Palestinian Talmud)*
Yal.	*Yalquṭ*
Yem. Targ.	*Yemenite Targum*

24.15   *Nag Hammadi Tractates*

Acts Pet. 12 Apost.	*Acts of Peter and the Twelve Apostles*
Allogenes	*Allogenes*
Ap. Jas	*Apocryphon of James*
Ap. John	*Apocryphon of John*
Apoc. Adam	*Apocalypse of Adam*
1 Apoc. Jas	*First Apocalypse of James*
2 Apoc. Jas.	*Second Apocalypse of James*
Apoc. Paul	*Apocalypse of Paul*
Apoc. Pet.	*Apocalypse of Peter*
Asclepius	*Asclepius 21–29*
Auth. Teach.	*Authoritative Teaching*
Dial. Sav.	*Dialogue of the Saviour*
Disc. 8–9	*Discourse on the Eighth and Ninth*
Ep. Pet. Phil.	*Letter of Peter to Philip*
Eugnostos	*Eugnostos the Blessed*
Exeg. Soul	*Exegesis on the Soul*
Gos. Eg.	*Gospel of the Egyptians*
Gos. Phil.	*Gospel of Philip*
Gos. Thom.	*Gospel of Thomas*
Gos. Truth	*Gospel of Truth*
Great Pow.	*Concept of our Great Power*
Hyp. Arch.	*Hypostasis of the Archons*
Hypsiph.	*Hypsiphrone*
Interp. Know.	*Interpretation of Knowledge*
Marsanes	*Marsanes*
Melch.	*Melchizedek*
Norea	*Thought of Norea*
On Bap. A, B, C	*On Baptism A, B, C*
On Euch. A, B	*On the Eucharist A, B*
Orig. World	*On the Origin of the World*
Paraph. Shem	*Paraphrase of Shem*
Pr. Paul	*Prayer of the Apostle Paul*
Pr. Thanks.	*Prayer of Thanksgiving*
Sent. Sextus	*Sentences of Sextus*
Soph. Jes. Chr.	*Sophia of Jesus Christ*
Steles Seth	*Three Steles of Seth*

Teach. Silv.	*Teachings of Silvanus*
Testim. Truth	*Testimony of Truth*
Thom. Cont.	*Book of Thomas the Contender*
Thund.	*Thunder, Perfect Mind*
Treat. Res.	*Treatise on Resurrection*
Treat. Seth	*Second Treatise of the Great Seth*
Tri. Trac.	*Tripartite Tractate*
Trim. Prot.	*Trimorphic Protennoia*
Val. Exp.	*A Valentinian Exposition*
Zost.	*Zostrianos*

25. ABBREVIATIONS OF PERIODICALS, REFERENCE WORKS AND SERIALS

25.1 The function of these abbreviations and acronyms is to save space and minimize the length of footnotes by abbreviating the names of commonly cited works. On the whole, SAP's rule is to require abbreviation of all works that appear in the following list; but for certain purposes (for example, when the book is addressed to an audience wider than that of professional biblical scholars) it is appropriate for all titles to be spelled out in full.

25.2 The general principle governing these abbreviations is that journals with more than one word in their title are abbreviated, as are multi-volume reference works and the names of series. On the whole, these abbreviations are the same as those adopted by the Society of Biblical Literature.

AASOR	Annual of the American Schools of Oriental Research
AB	Anchor Bible
ABD	David Noel Freedman (ed.), *The Anchor Bible Dictionary* (New York: Doubleday, 1992)
AbrN	*Abr-Nahrain*
AcOr	*Acta orientalia*
ADAJ	*Annual of the Department of Antiquities of Jordan*
Aeg	*Aegyptus*
AER	*American Ecclesiastical Review*
AfO	*Archiv für Orientforschung*
AGJU	Arbeiten zur Geschichte des antiken Judentums und des Urchristentums
AHw	Wolfram von Soden, *Akkadisches Handwörterbuch* (Wiesbaden: Harrassowitz, 1959–81)
AION	*Annali dell'istituto orientale di Napoli*
AJA	*American Journal of Archaeology*
AJBA	*Australian Journal of Biblical Archaeology*
AJP	*American Journal of Philology*
AJSL	*American Journal of Semitic Languages and Literatures*

AJT	American Journal of Theology
ALBO	Analecta lovaniensia biblica et orientalia
ALGHJ	Arbeiten zur Literatur und Geschichte des hellenistischen Judentums
ALUOS	Annual of Leeds University Oriental Society
AnBib	Analecta biblica
AnBoll	Analecta Bollandiana
ANEP	James B. Pritchard (ed.), *Ancient Near East in Pictures Relating to the Old Testament* (Princeton: Princeton University Press, 1954)
ANET	James B. Pritchard (ed.), *Ancient Near Eastern Texts Relating to the Old Testament* (Princeton: Princeton University Press, 1950)
ANF	Anti-Nicene Fathers
Ang	*Angelicum*
AnOr	Analecta orientalia
ANQ	*Andover Newton Quarterly*
ANRW	Hildegard Temporini and Wolfgang Haase (eds.), *Aufstieg und Niedergang der römischen Welt: Geschichte und Kultur Roms im Spiegel der neueren Forschung* (Berlin: W. de Gruyter, 1972–)
ANTJ	Arbeiten zum Neuen Testament und Judentum
Anton	*Antonianum*
AOAT	Alter Orient und Altes Testament
AOS	American Oriental Series
APOT	R.H. Charles (ed.), *Apocrypha and Pseudepigrapha of the Old Testament in English* (2 vols.; Oxford: Clarendon Press, 1913)
ARG	*Archiv für Reformationsgeschichte*
ARM	Archives royales de Mari
ArOr	*Archiv orientální*
ARW	*Archiv für Religionswissenschaft*
ASNU	Acta seminarii neotestamentici upsaliensis
AsSeign	*Assemblées du Seigneur*
ASTI	*Annual of the Swedish Theological Institute*
ATAbh	Alttestamentliche Abhandlungen
ATANT	Abhandlungen zur Theologie des Alten und Neuen Testaments
ATD	Das Alte Testament Deutsch
ATR	*Anglican Theological Review*
AusBR	*Australian Biblical Review*
AUSS	*Andrews University Seminary Studies*
AV	Authorized Version
BA	*Biblical Archaeologist*
BAC	Biblioteca de autores cristianos

BAGD	Walter Bauer, William F. Arndt, F. William Gingrich and Frederick W. Danker, *A Greek–English Lexicon of the New Testament and Other Early Christian Literature* (Chicago: University of Chicago Press, 2nd edn, 1958)
BARev	*Biblical Archaeology Review*
BASOR	*Bulletin of the American Schools of Oriental Research*
BASORSup	*Bulletin of the American Schools of Oriental Research*, Supplements
BBB	Bonner biblische Beiträge
BCSR	*Bulletin of the Council on the Study of Religion*
BDB	Francis Brown, S.R. Driver and Charles A. Briggs, *A Hebrew and English Lexicon of the Old Testament* (Oxford: Clarendon Press, 1907)
BDF	Friedrich Blass, A. Debrunner and Robert W. Funk, *A Greek Grammar of the New Testament and Other Early Christian Literature* (Cambridge: Cambridge University Press, 1961)
BDR	Friedrich Blass, Albert Debrunner and Friedrich Rehkopf, *Grammatik des neutestamentlichen Griechisch* (Göttingen: Vandenhoeck & Ruprecht, 16th edn, 1984 [and other editions])
BeO	*Bibbia e oriente*
BETL	Bibliotheca ephemeridum theologicarum lovaniensium
BEvT	Beiträge zur evangelischen Theologie
BFCT	Beiträge zur Förderung christlicher Theologie
BHK	R. Kittel (ed.), *Biblia hebraica* (Stuttgart: Württembergische Bibelanstalt, 1937)
BHS	*Biblia hebraica stuttgartensia*
BHT	Beiträge zur historischen Theologie
Bib	*Biblica*
BibB	Biblische Beiträge
BibInt	*Biblical Interpretation: A Journal of Contemporary Approaches*
BibLeb	*Bibel und Leben*
Biblicon	*Biblicon*
BibOr	Biblica et orientalia
BIES	*Bulletin of the Israel Exploration Society* (= *Yediot*)
BIFAO	*Bulletin de l'Institut français d'archéologie orientale*
BIOSCS	*Bulletin of the International Organization for Septuagint and Cognate Studies*
BJPES	*Bulletin of the Jewish Palestine Exploration Society*

BJRL	*Bulletin of the John Rylands University Library of Manchester*
BJS	Brown Judaic Studies
BK	*Bibel und Kirche*
BKAT	Biblischer Kommentar: Altes Testament
BLE	*Bulletin de littérature ecclésiastique*
BLit	*Bibel und Liturgie*
BN	*Biblische Notizen*
BNTC	Black's New Testament Commentaries
BO	*Bibliotheca orientalis*
BibRes	*Biblical Research*
BR	*Bible Review*
BSac	*Bibliotheca Sacra*
BSO(A)S	*Bulletin of the School of Oriental (and African) Studies*
BT	*The Bible Translator*
BTB	*Biblical Theology Bulletin*
BTS	*Bible et terre sainte*
BVC	*Bible et vie chrétienne*
BWANT	Beiträge zur Wissenschaft vom Alten und Neuen Testament
BZ	*Biblische Zeitschrift*
BZAW	Beihefte zur *ZAW*
BZNW	Beihefte zur *ZNW*
BZRGG	Beihefte zur *ZRGG*
CAD	Ignace I. Gelb *et al.* (eds.), *The Assyrian Dictionary of the Oriental Institute of the University of Chicago* (Chicago: Oriental Institute, 1964–)
CAH	Cambridge Ancient History
CAT	Commentaire de l'Ancien Testament
CB	*Cultura bíblica*
CBQ	*Catholic Biblical Quarterly*
CBQMS	*Catholic Biblical Quarterly*, Monograph Series
CCath	Corpus Catholicorum
CChr	Corpus Christianorum
CGTC	Cambridge Greek Testament Commentary
CH	*Church History*
CHR	*Catholic Historical Review*
CIG	*Corpus inscriptionum graecarum*
CII	*Corpus inscriptionum iudaicarum*
CIL	*Corpus inscriptionum latinarum*
CIS	*Corpus inscriptionum semiticarum*
CJT	*Canadian Journal of Theology*
ClQ	*Classical Quarterly*
CNT	Commentaire du Nouveau Testament

ConBNT	Coniectanea biblica, New Testament
ConBOT	Coniectanea biblica, Old Testament
ConNT	*Coniectanea neotestamentica*
CQ	*Church Quarterly*
CQR	*Church Quarterly Review*
CR	*Critical Review of Books in Religion*
CRBS	*Currents in Research: Biblical Studies*
CRAIBL	*Comptes rendus de l'Académie des inscriptions et belles-lettres*
CRINT	Compendia rerum iudaicarum ad Novum Testamentum
CSCO	Corpus scriptorum christianorum orientalium
CSEL	Corpus scriptorum ecclesiasticorum latinorum
CSRBull	*Council on the Study of Religion Bulletin*
CTA	A. Herdner (ed.), *Corpus des tablettes en cunéiformes alphabétiques découvertes à Ras Shamra–Ugarit de 1929 à 1939* (Paris: Imprimerie nationale Geuthner, 1963)
CTM	*Concordia Theological Monthly*
CurTM	*Currents in Theology and Mission*
DACL	*Dictionnaire d'archéologie chrétienne et de liturgie*
DBSup	*Dictionnaire de la Bible, Supplément*
DISO	Charles-F. Jean and Jacob Hoftijzer (eds.), *Dictionnaire des inscriptions sémitiques de l'ouest* (Leiden: E.J. Brill, 1965)
DJD	Discoveries in the Judaean Desert
DOTT	D. Winton Thomas (ed.), *Documents from Old Testament Times* (London: Nelson, 1958)
DTC	*Dictionnaire de théologie catholique*
DTT	*Dansk teologisk tidsskrift*
EBib	Etudes bibliques
EHAT	Exegetisches Handbuch zum Alten Testament
EKKNT	Evangelisch-Katholischer Kommentar zum Neuen Testament
EncJud	*Encyclopaedia Judaica*
EnchBib	*Enchiridion biblicum*
EstBíb	*Estudios bíblicos*
ETL	*Ephemerides theologicae lovanienses*
ETR	*Etudes théologiques et religieuses*
EvK	Evangelische Kommentare
EvQ	*Evangelical Quarterly*
EvT	*Evangelische Theologie*
ExpTim	*Expository Times*
FemTh	*Feminist Theology*
FFNT	Foundations and Facets: New Testament

FN	*Filología neotestamentaria*
FzB	Forschung zur Bibel
FOTL	The Forms of the Old Testament Literature
FRLANT	Forschungen zur Religion und Literatur des Alten und Neuen Testaments
GCS	Griechische christliche Schriftsteller
GKB	Wilhelm Gesenius, E. Kautzsch and Gotthelf Bergsträsser, *Hebräische Grammatik* (Hildesheim: G. Olms, 28th edn, 1962)
GKC	*Gesenius' Hebrew Grammar* (ed. E. Kautzsch, revised and trans. A.E. Cowley; Oxford: Clarendon Press, 1910)
GRBS	*Greek, Roman, and Byzantine Studies*
GTJ	*Grace Theological Journal*
Greg	*Gregorianum*
HALAT	Ludwig Koehler *et al.* (eds.), *Hebräisches und aramäisches Lexikon zum Alten Testament* (5 vols.; Leiden: E.J. Brill, 1967–1995)
HAR	*Hebrew Annual Review*
HAT	Handbuch zum Alten Testament
HBT	*Horizons in Biblical Theology*
HDB	James Hastings (ed.), *A Dictionary of the Bible* (5 vols.; New York: Charles Scribner's Sons, 1898–1904)
HDR	Harvard Dissertations in Religion
HeyJ	*Heythrop Journal*
HibJ	*Hibbert Journal*
HKAT	Handkommentar zum Alten Testament
HKNT	Handkommentar zum Neuen Testament
HNT	Handbuch zum Neuen Testament
HNTC	Harper's NT Commentaries
HR	*History of Religions*
HSM	Harvard Semitic Monographs
HTKNT	Herders theologischer Kommentar zum Neuen Testament
HTR	*Harvard Theological Review*
HUCA	*Hebrew Union College Annual*
HZ	*Historische Zeitschrift*
IB	*Interpreter's Bible*
IBS	*Irish Biblical Studies*
ICC	International Critical Commentary
IDB	George Arthur Buttrick (ed.), *The Interpreter's Dictionary of the Bible* (4 vols.; Nashville: Abingdon Press, 1962)
IDBSup	*IDB*, Supplementary Volume

IEJ	*Israel Exploration Journal*
Int	*Interpretation*
ISBE	Geoffrey Bromiley (ed.), *The International Standard Bible Encyclopedia* (4 vols.; Grand Rapids: Eerdmans, rev. edn, 1979–88)
ITQ	*Irish Theological Quarterly*
JA	*Journal asiatique*
JAAR	*Journal of the American Academy of Religion*
JAC	*Jahrbuch für Antike und Christentum*
JANESCU	*Journal of the Ancient Near Eastern Society of Columbia University*
JAOS	*Journal of the American Oriental Society*
JB	*Jerusalem Bible*
JBL	*Journal of Biblical Literature*
JBR	*Journal of Bible and Religion*
JewEnc	*The Jewish Encyclopedia*
JCS	*Journal of Cuneiform Studies*
JEA	*Journal of Egyptian Archaeology*
JEH	*Journal of Ecclesiastical History*
JEOL	*Jaarbericht . . . ex oriente lux*
JES	*Journal of Ecumenical Studies*
JETS	*Journal of the Evangelical Theological Society*
JFSR	*Journal of Feminist Studies in Religion*
JHS	*Journal of Hellenic Studies*
JJS	*Journal of Jewish Studies*
JMA	*Journal of Mediterranean Archaeology*
JNES	*Journal of Near Eastern Studies*
JNSL	*Journal of Northwest Semitic Languages*
JPJ	*Journal of Progressive Judaism*
JPOS	*Journal of the Palestine Oriental Society*
JPSV	*Jewish Publication Society Version*
JPT	*Journal of Pentecostal Theology*
JPTSup	*Journal of Pentecostal Theology*, Supplement Series
JQR	*Jewish Quarterly Review*
JQRMS	*Jewish Quarterly Review*, Monograph Series
JR	*Journal of Religion*
JRAS	*Journal of the Royal Asiatic Society*
JRE	*Journal of Religious Ethics*
JRelS	*Journal of Religious Studies*
JRH	*Journal of Religious History*
JRS	*Journal of Roman Studies*
JRT	*Journal of Religious Thought*
JSHRZ	Jüdische Schriften aus hellenistisch-römischer Zeit
JSJ	*Journal for the Study of Judaism in the Persian, Hellenistic and Roman Period*

JSNT	*Journal for the Study of the New Testament*
JSNTSup	*Journal for the Study of the New Testament, Supplement Series*
JSOT	*Journal for the Study of the Old Testament*
JSOTSup	*Journal for the Study of the Old Testament, Supplement Series*
JSP	*Journal for the Study of the Pseudepigrapha*
JSPSup	*Journal for the Study of the Pseudepigrapha, Supplement Series*
JSS	*Journal of Semitic Studies*
JSSR	*Journal for the Scientific Study of Religion*
JTC	*Journal for Theology and the Church*
JTS	*Journal of Theological Studies*
Judaica	*Judaica: Beiträge zum Verständnis des jüdischen Schicksals in Vergangenheit und Gegenwart*
KAI	H. Donner and W. Röllig, *Kanaanäische und aramäische Inschriften* (3 vols.; Wiesbaden: Harrassowitz, 1962–64)
KAT	Kommentar zum Alten Testament
KB	Ludwig Koehler and Walter Baumgartner (eds.), *Lexicon in Veteris Testamenti libros* (Leiden: E.J. Brill, 1953)
KD	*Kerygma und Dogma*
KHAT	Kurzer Hand-Kommentar zum Alten Testament
KJV	King James Version
LB	*Linguistica biblica*
LCC	Library of Christian Classics
LCL	Loeb Classical Library
LD	Lectio divina
Leš	*Lešonénu*
LPGL	G.W.H. Lampe, *A Patristic Greek Lexicon* (Oxford: Clarendon Press, 1961)
LQ	*Lutheran Quarterly*
LR	*Lutherische Rundschau*
LSJ	H.G. Liddell, Robert Scott and H. Stuart Jones, *Greek–English Lexicon* (Oxford: Clarendon Press, 9th edn, 1968)
LTK	*Lexikon für Theologie und Kirche*
LUÅ	Lunds universitets årsskrift
LW	*Lutheran World*
MDOG	Mitteilungen der deutschen Orient-Gesellschaft
MeyerK	H.A.W. Meyer (ed.), Kritisch-exegetischer Kommentar über das Neue Testament [sometimes referred to as KEK]

MGWJ	*Monatsschrift für Geschichte und Wissenschaft des Judentums*
MMA	Monographs in Mediterranean Archaeology
MNTC	Moffatt NT Commentary
MScRel	*Mélanges de science religieuse*
MTZ	*Münchener theologische Zeitschrift*
MUSJ	*Mélanges de l'université Saint-Joseph*
MVAG	Mitteilungen der vorderasiatisch-ägyptischen Gesellschaft
NAB	*New American Bible*
NASB	*New American Standard Bible*
NCB	New Century Bible
NEB	*New English Bible*
NedTTs	*Nederlands theologisch tijdschrift*
Neot	*Neotestamentica*
NHS	Nag Hammadi Studies
NICNT	New International Commentary on the New Testament
NICOT	New International Commentary on the Old Testament
NIDOTE	Willem A. VanGemeren (ed.), *New International Dictionary of Old Testament Theology and Exegesis* (5 vols.; Grand Rapids: Zondervan, 1997)
NIDNTT	Colin Brown (ed.), *The New International Dictionary of New Testament Theology* (3 vols.; Exeter: Paternoster Press, 1975)
NIGTC	The New International Greek Testament Commentary
NIV	New International Version
NJB	*New Jerusalem Bible*
NKZ	*Neue kirchliche Zeitschrift*
NorTT	*Norsk Teologisk Tidsskrift*
NovT	*Novum Testamentum*
NovTSup	*Novum Testamentum*, Supplements
NPNF	Nicene and Post-Nicene Fathers
NRSV	New Revised Standard Version
NRT	*La nouvelle revue théologique*
NTA	*New Testament Abstracts*
NTAbh	Neutestamentliche Abhandlungen
NTD	Das Neue Testament Deutsch
NTG	New Testament Guides
NTL	New Testament Library
NTOA	Novum Testamentum et orbis antiquus
NTS	*New Testament Studies*
NTTS	New Testament Tools and Studies

Numen	*Numen: International Review for the History of Religions*
OBO	Orbis biblicus et orientalis
OCD	*Oxford Classical Dictionary*
OLP	Orientalia lovaniensia periodica
OLZ	*Orientalistische Literaturzeitung*
Or	*Orientalia*
OrAnt	*Oriens antiquus*
OrChr	*Oriens christianus*
OrSyr	*L'orient syrien*
OTA	*Old Testament Abstracts*
OTG	Old Testament Guides
OTL	Old Testament Library
OTP	James Charlesworth (ed.), *Old Testament Pseudepigrapha*
OTS	*Oudtestamentische Studiën*
PAAJR	*Proceedings of the American Academy of Jewish Research*
PEFQS	*Palestine Exploration Fund, Quarterly Statement*
PEQ	*Palestine Exploration Quarterly*
PG	J.-P. Migne (ed.), *Patrologia cursus completa... Series graeca* (166 vols.; Paris: Petit-Montrouge, 1857–83)
PGM	K. Preisendanz (ed.), *Papyri graecae magicae*
PJ	*Palästina-Jahrbuch*
PL	J.-P. Migne (ed.), *Patrologia cursus completus... Series prima [latina]* (221 vols.; Paris: J.-P. Migne, 1844–65)
PO	Patrologia orientalis
PRU	*Le palais royal d'Ugarit*
P(ST)J	*Perkins (School of Theology) Journal*
PTMS	Pittsburgh Theological Monograph Series
PVTG	Pseudepigrapha Veteris Testamenti graece
P W	August Friedrich von Pauly and Georg Wissowa (eds.), *Real-Encyclopädie der classischen Altertumswissenschaft* (Stuttgart: Metzler, 1894–)
PWSup	Supplement to PW
QDAP	*Quarterly of the Department of Antiquities in Palestine*
RA	*Revue d'assyriologie et d'archéologie orientale*
RAC	*Reallexikon für Antike und Christentum*
RArch	*Revue archéologique*
RB	*Revue biblique*
RBén	*Revue bénédictine*
RCB	*Revista de cultura bíblica*

RE	*Realencyklopädie für protestantische Theologie und Kirche*
RechBib	Recherches bibliques
REg	*Revue d'égyptologie*
REJ	*Revue des études juives*
Rel	*Religion*
RelS	*Religious Studies*
RelSRev	*Religious Studies Review*
ResQ	*Restoration Quarterly*
RevExp	*Review and Expositor*
RevistB	*Revista biblica*
RevQ	*Revue de Qumran*
RevScRel	*Revue des sciences religieuses*
RevSém	*Revue sémitique*
RevThom	*Revue thomiste*
RGG	*Religion in Geschichte und Gegenwart*
RHE	*Revue d'histoire ecclésiastique*
RHPR	*Revue d'histoire et de philosophie religieuses*
RHR	*Revue de l'histoire des religions*
RivB	*Rivista biblica*
RNT	Regensburger Neues Testament
RRR	*Renaissance and Reformation Review*
RSN	*Religious Studies News*
RSO	*Rivista degli studi orientali*
RSPT	*Revue des sciences philosophiques et théologiques*
RSR	*Recherches de science religieuse*
RSV	Revised Standard Version
RTL	*Revue théologique de Louvain*
RTP	*Revue de théologie et de philosophie*
RTR	*Reformed Theological Review*
RV	Revised Version
SAM	Sheffield Archaeological Monographs
SANT	Studien zum Alten und Neuen Testament
SB	Sources bibliques
SBB	Stuttgarter biblische Beiträge
SBFLA	*Studii biblici franciscani liber annuus*
SBL	Society of Biblical Literature
SBLASP	SBL Abstracts and Seminar Papers
SBLDS	SBL Dissertation Series
SBLMasS	SBL Masoretic Studies
SBLMS	SBL Monograph Series
SBLRBS	SBL Resources for Biblical Study
SBLSBS	SBL Sources for Biblical Study
SBLSCS	SBL Septuagint and Cognate Studies
SBLSP	SBL Seminar Papers

SBLSS	SBL Semeia Studies
SBLTT	SBL Texts and Translations
SBM	Stuttgarter biblische Monographien
SBS	Stuttgarter Bibelstudien
SBT	Studies in Biblical Theology
SC	Sources chrétiennes
SCHNT	Studia ad corpus hellenisticum Novi Testamenti
ScEs	*Science et esprit*
Scr	*Scripture*
ScrB	*Scripture Bulletin*
SE	*Studia Evangelica I, II, III* (= TU 73 [1959], 87 [1964], 88 [1964], etc.)
SEARCH	Sheffield Environmental and Archaeological Research Campaign in the Hebrides
SEÅ	*Svensk exegetisk årsbok*
SecCent	*Second Century*
Sef	*Sefarad*
Sem	*Semitica*
SER	Sheffield Excavation Reports
SJ	Studia judaica
SJLA	Studies in Judaism in Late Antiquity
SJOT	*Scandinavian Journal of the Old Testament*
SJT	*Scottish Journal of Theology*
SNT	Studien zum Neuen Testament
SNTSMS	Society for New Testament Studies Monograph Series
SNTU	Studien zum Neuen Testament und seiner Umwelt
SOTSMS	Society for Old Testament Study Monograph Series
SPap	*Studia papyrologica*
SPAW	Sitzungsberichte der preussischen Akademie der Wissenschaften
SPB	Studia postbiblica
SR	*Studies in Religion/Sciences religieuses*
ST	*Studia theologica*
STÅ	*Svensk teologisk årsskrift*
STDJ	Studies on the Texts of the Desert of Judah
STK	*Svensk teologisk kvartalskrift*
Str–B	[Hermann L. Strack and] Paul Billerbeck, *Kommentar zum Neuen Testament aus Talmud und Midrasch* (7 vols.; Munich: Beck, 1922–61)
StudNeot	Studia neotestamentica
StudOr	Studia orientalia
SUNT	Studien zur Umwelt des Neuen Testaments
SVTP	Studia in Veteris Testamenti pseudepigrapha
SymBU	Symbolae biblicae upsalienses

TAPA	*Transactions of the American Philological Association*
TBl	*Theologische Blätter*
TBü	Theologische Bücherei
TBT	*The Bible Today*
TD	*Theology Digest*
TDNT	Gerhard Kittel and Gerhard Friedrich (eds.), *Theological Dictionary of the New Testament* (trans. Geoffrey W. Bromiley; 10 vols.; Grand Rapids: Eerdmans, 1964–)
TDOT	G.J. Botterweck and H. Ringgren (eds.), *Theological Dictionary of the Old Testament*
TEV	Today's English Version
TF	*Theologische Forschung*
TGl	*Theologie und Glaube*
THAT	Ernst Jenni and Claus Westermann (eds.), *Theologisches Handwörterbuch zum Alten Testament* (Munich: Chr. Kaiser, 1971–76)
TheolSex	*Theology and Sexuality*
THKNT	Theologischer Handkommentar zum Neuen Testament
ThWAT	G.J. Botterweck and H. Ringgren (eds.), *Theologisches Wörterbuch zum Alten Testament* (Stuttgart: W. Kohlhammer, 1970–)
TLZ	*Theologische Literaturzeitung*
TNTC	Tyndale New Testament Commentaries
TOTC	Tyndale Old Testament Commentaries
TP	*Theologie und Philosophie*
TPQ	*Theologisch-praktische Quartalschrift*
TQ	*Theologische Quartalschrift*
TRE	*Theologische Realenzyklopädie*
TRev	*Theologische Revue*
TRu	*Theologische Rundschau*
TS	*Theological Studies*
TSK	*Theologische Studien und Kritiken*
TT	*Teologisk Tidsskrift*
TTod	*Theology Today*
TTZ	*Trierer theologische Zeitschrift*
TU	Texte und Untersuchungen
TWNT	Gerhard Kittel and Gerhard Friedrich (eds.), *Theologisches Wörterbuch zum Neuen Testament* (11 vols.; Stuttgart, Kohlhammer, 1932–79)

TWOT	R. Laird Harris, Gleason L. Archer, Jr and Bruce K. Waltke (eds.), *Theological Wordbook of the Old Testament* (2 vols.; Chicago: Moody Press, 1980)
TynBul	*Tyndale Bulletin*
TNTC	Tyndale New Testament Commentaries
TOTC	Tyndale Old Testament Commentaries
TZ	*Theologische Zeitschrift*
UBSGNT	United Bible Societies' *Greek New Testament*
UF	*Ugarit-Forschungen*
UNT	Untersuchungen zum Neuen Testament
US	*Una Sancta*
USQR	*Union Seminary Quarterly Review*
UT	Cyrus H. Gordon, *Ugaritic Textbook* (Analecta orientalia, 38; Rome: Pontifical Biblical Institute Press, 1965)
UUÅ	Uppsala universitetsårsskrift
VC	*Vigiliae christianae*
VCaro	*Verbum caro*
VD	*Verbum domini*
VF	*Verkündigung und Forschung*
V S	Verbum salutis
VSpir	*Vie spirituelle*
V T	*Vetus Testamentun*
VTSup	*Vetus Testamentum*, Supplements
W A	M. Luther, *Kritische Gesamtausgabe* (= 'Weimar' edition)
WBC	Word Biblical Commentary
WMANT	Wissenschaftliche Monographien zum Alten und Neuen Testament
WO	*Die Welt des Orients*
WTJ	*Westminster Theological Journal*
WUNT	Wissenschaftliche Untersuchungen zum Neuen Testament
W W	*Word and World*
WZKM	*Wiener Zeitschrift für die Kunde des Morgenlandes*
ZA	*Zeitschrift für Assyriologie*
ZAH	*Zeitschrift für Althebraistik*
Z A W	*Zeitschrift für die alttestamentliche Wissenschaft*
ZDMG	*Zeitschrift der deutschen morgenländischen Gesellschaft*
ZDPV	*Zeitschrift des deutschen Palästina-Vereins*
ZHT	*Zeitschrift für historische Theologie*
ZKG	*Zeitschrift für Kirchengeschichte*
ZKT	*Zeitschrift für katholische Theologie*

ZMR	*Zeitschrift für Missionskunde und Religionswissenschaft*
ZNW	*Zeitschrift für die neutestamentliche Wissenschaft*
ZPE	*Zeitschrift für Papyrologie und Epigraphik*
ZRGG	*Zeitschrift für Religions- und Geistesgeschichte*
ZST	*Zeitschrift für systematische Theologie*
ZTK	*Zeitschrift für Theologie und Kirche*
ZWT	*Zeitschrift für wissenschaftliche Theologie*

26. BIBLICAL REFERENCE FORMS
USED BY OTHER JOURNALS

26.1 There are many possible forms of reference to biblical texts. The learned journals display a great variety. Though it is not a matter of the highest importance, it is a good policy to use the exact form of reference that is to be found in one's source, and it is SAP's practice to follow the style of the journal that is being cited. The table below allows authors and editors to check, at least for some of the principal journals in biblical studies, whether the form in the cited source has been reproduced correctly.

26.2 The table must, however, be used with caution, since it is a rare journal that has adhered to a consistent style throughout its history. The following factors make the table less than wholly reliable: (1) Some journals do not impose a single form of reference; in such cases, the form that seems to be most common has been noted and 'etc.' has been added in the last column. (2) Different styles are used by authors and editors in different languages, and some international journals display many varieties of reference; in such cases the form cited is the form used in articles in the language most commonly used in the journal. (3) The transition between one form and another rarely happens at a single moment; articles get set in type at various points in the course of production of an issue of a journal, and there is usually a great deal of inconsistency at the time of a change of style.

26.3 Despite those caveats, the table can serve as a useful check on the probability that the form of a particular reference is correct. If the form in one's text corresponds to the form registered below, one can be fairly sure that the reference is correct; but one should not hastily conclude that a difference from the form below indicates that a mistake has been made, especially if the form in one's text corresponds with a form previously in use in the particular journal.

Bib	1 (1920)	II Cor. 3, 7	
	39 (1958)	II Cor 3,7	
	43 (1962)	2 Cor 3,7	
B A	1 (1938)	2 Cor 3:7	
BibInt	1 (1992)	2 Cor. 3:7	
BZ	1 (1957)	2 Cor 3, 7	
	25 (1981)	2 Cor 3,7	
CBQ	1 (1938)	2 Cor 3,7	
	33 (1971)	2 Cor 3:7	
ExpT	1 (1899–90)	II Cor. iii.7	
	10 (1898–99)	2 Cor 3^7	
	97 (1985–86)	2 Cor 3:7	
Henoch	1 (1979)	*II Cor.* 3,7	
Int	1 (1956)	II Cor. 3:7	
JBL	39 (1920)	II Cor. 3 7	
	56 (1937)	II Cor 3 7	
	90 (1971)	II Cor 3:7	
	91 (1972)	2 Cor 3:7	
JJS	1 (1949)	*2 Cor.* 3:7	etc.
	31 (1980)	2 Cor. 3:7	
JSS	1 (1949)	*2 Cor.* 3:7	
	31 (1980)	2 Cor. 3:7	
JSJ	1 (1970)	2 Cor. 3, 7	etc.
JSNT	1 (1978)	2 Cor. 3:7	etc.
	19 (1983)	2 Cor. 3.7	
JSOT	1 (1976)	2 Cor. 3:7	etc.
	26 (1983)	2 Cor. 3.7	
JTS	1 (1900)	II Cor. iii 7	
	NS 1 (1950)	II Cor. 3^7	
	5 (1954)	II Cor. iii. 7	
	38 (1987)	II Cor. 3: 7	
NTS	1 (1954–55)	II Cor. iii. 7	
	26 (1980)	II Cor. 3. 7	
	28 (1982)	2 Cor. 3. 7	
	31 (1985)	2 Cor 3. 7	
R B	55 (1948)	*II Cor.* III, 7	
	59 (1952)	*II Cor.,* III, 7	
	94 (1987)	2 Co 3, 7	
VT	1 (1951)	2 Cor. iii 7	
ZAW	50 (1932)	II Cor 3 7	
	97 (1985)	II Cor 3,7	

27. Publishers' Names

27.1 This is a list of the names and the principal locations of publishers who are most commonly referred to in scholarly works on biblical studies.

27.2 When a publisher has more than one office, only the first stated or the one presumed to be the head office is noted as the place of publication in the Bibliography and footnote references.

27.3 The name of a publisher includes 'Press' if it is part of the name, but not terms denoting the legal status of the company, such as Ltd or Co. or Inc. (except where listed hereunder).

27.4 When there are two elements in a publisher's name, they are usually joined by & (ampersand) or – (en-dash); thus

T. & T. Clark	Augsburg–Fortress
George Allen & Unwin	McGraw–Hill
Letouzey & Ané	Prentice–Hall

27.5 Publishers and primary places of publication:

Abingdon Press (Nashville *or* New York)
Abingdon–Cokesbury (New York)
Åbo Akademi (Åbo)
Academic Press (London *or* New York)
Academy for Jewish Research (Jerusalem)
Akademie Verlag (Berlin)
Akademische Verlagsbuchhandlung (Freiburg)
Alba House (New York)
George Allen & Unwin (London)
Allenson (Naperville, IL)
Almond Press (Sheffield)

American Oriental Society (New Haven)
American Schools of Oriental Research (Cambridge, MA)
Archon Books (Hamden, CT)
Armstrong & Son (New York)
Edward Arnold (London)
Aschendorff (Münster)
Association Press (New York)
Athlone Press (London)
Attic Press (Greenwood, SC)
Attinger (Neuchâtel)
Augsburg (Minneapolis)
Augsburg–Fortress (Minneapolis)
Stephen Austin & Sons (Hertford)

Baker Book House (Grand Rapids)

Bamberger & Wahrmann (Jerusalem)

Banner of Truth Trust (London *or* Carlisle, PA)

Barrie & Jenkins (London)

Basic Books (New York)

Beacon Press (Boston)

Beauchesne (Paris)

Beck (Munich)

Beltz Athenäum (Weinheim)

Benjamin/Cummings (Menlo Park, CA)

Benzinger Verlag (Zürich)

Berchthold Haller (Bern)

C. Bertelsmann (Gütersloh)

Bethany (Minneapolis)

Biblical Institute Press (Rome)

A. & C. Black (London)

Basil Blackwell (Oxford)

Bloch Publishing Co. (New York)

Bobbs–Merrill (New York)

Bookman Associates (New York)

Bouvier (Bonn)

George Braziller (New York)

E.J. Brill (Leiden)

The British Academy (London)

Brockhaus (Wuppertal)

Calwer Verlag (Stuttgart)

Cambridge University Press (Cambridge)

John Carroll University Press (Wilmington, DE)

Carta (Jerusalem)

Case Western Reserve University Press (Cleveland)

Cassell, Petter, Galpin & Co. (London)

Catholic Biblical Association (Washington)

Catholic University of America Press (Washington)

Cerf (Paris)

Geoffrey Chapman (London)

Clarendon Press (Oxford)

T. & T. Clark (Edinburgh)

Cokesburg (Nashville)

Collins (London)

Columbia University Press (New York)

Consejo Superior de Investigaciones Cientificas (Madrid)

Cornell University Press (Ithaca, NY)

Crossroad (New York)

Darton, Longman & Todd (London)

Deichert (Leipzig)

Dekker & Van de Vegt (Nijmegen)

Delachaux & Niestlé (Neuchâtel *or* Paris)

Desclée de Brouwer (Paris)

Deutsche Bibelgesellschaft (Stuttgart)

Doubleday (Garden City, NY *or* New York)

Gerald Duckworth (London)

Duculot (Gembloux)

Duke University Press (Durham, NC)

Duquesne University Press (Pittsburgh)

Dura-Europos Publications (New Haven)

Jacob Dybwad (Oslo)

Echter Verlag (Würzburg)

Edinburgh University Press (Edinburgh)

Editrice Anselmiana (Rome)

Editrice Pontificia Università Gregoriana (Rome)

Eerdmans (Grand Rapids)

Egypt Exploration Fund (London)

Eisenbrauns (Winona Lake, IN)

Epworth Press (London)

Evangelische Verlagsanstalt (Berlin)
Evangelischer Verlag (Zollikon–Zürich)
EVZ-Verlag (Zürich)

Feldheim (Jerusalem *or* Spring Valley, NY)
Fortress Press (Philadelphia)
Franciscan Herald Press (Chicago)
Franciscan Printing Press (Jerusalem)
Free Press (Glencoe)
Funk & Wagnalls (New York)

J. Gabalda (Paris)
G.E.C. Gad (Copenhagen)
Gelbstverlag der Erben (Berlin)
Gerstenberg (Hildesheim)
Michael Glazier (Wilmington, DE)
C.W.K. Gleerup (Lund)
Gregorian University Press (Rome)
W. de Gruyter (Berlin)
Gütersloher Verlagshaus (Gütersloh)

Peter Hanstein (Bonn *or* Cologne)
Harcourt Brace Jovanovich (New York)
Harcourt, Brace & World (New York)
Harcourt, Brace & Company (New York)
HarperCollins (New York *or* London)
HarperSanFrancisco (San Francisco)
Harper & Brothers (New York)
Harper & Row (New York *or* San Francisco)
Otto Harrassowitz (Leipzig *or* Wiesbaden)
Hartford Seminary Foundation

Press (Hartford, CT)
Harvard University Press (Cambridge, MA)
Hebrew Union College Press (Cincinnati)
Heinemann (London)
Hendrickson (Peabody, MA)
Herald Press (Kitchener, Ontario)
Herder & Herder (New York)
Herder (Freiburg *or* Rome)
Hermon Press (New York)
Wilhelm Hertz (Berlin)
J.C. Hinrichs (Leipzig)
Hodder & Stoughton (London)
Holt, Rinehart & Winston (New York)
Huber (Munich *or* Frauenfeld)
Humanities Press (New York)
Hutchinson (London)

Indiana University Press (Bloomington)
Institut Biblique Pontifical (Rome) [use Pontifical Biblical Institute]
Inter-Varsity Press (Leicester *or* London)
InterVarsity Press (Downers Grove, IL)
Irish University Press (Shannon)
Itzkowski (Berlin)
IVP (Downers Grove, IL *or* Leicester)

Jewish Publication Society of America (Philadelphia)
Jewish Theological Seminary of America (New York)
Jewish Theological Society of America (New York)
John Knox Press (Atlanta *or* Richmond, VA)
The Johns Hopkins University Press (Baltimore *or* London)
JSOT Press (Sheffield)
Judson Press (Valley Forge, PA)

Chr. Kaiser Verlag (Munich *or*
    Gütersloh)
Katholisches Bibelwerk (Stuttgart)
J. Kauffmann (Frankfurt)
KBW (Stuttgart)
Keter Publishing House
    (Jerusalem)
Kiryath Sepher (Jerusalem)
John Knox Press (Atlanta *or*
    Richmond, VA)
W. Kohlhammer (Stuttgart)
Kok (Kampen)
Rabbi Kook Foundation
    (Jerusalem)
Kösel (Munich)
Kregel (Grand Rapids)
Ktav (New York)

Peter Lang (New York *or* Bern)
Librairie Lecoffre (Paris)
Leroux (Paris)
Letouzey & Ané (Paris)
Leuven University Press
    (Gembloux *or* Leuven)
Little, Brown & Co. (Boston)
Liturgical Press (Collegeville, MN)
Longmans, Green & Co. (London)
Longmans, Green (London *or*
    New York)
Louisiana State University Press
    (Baton Rouge)
Lundeqvist (Uppsala)
Lutterworth (London)

Machbarot Lesifrut (Tel Aviv)
Macmillan (London *or* New York)
Magnes Press (Jerusalem)
Makor (Jerusalem)
Manchester University Press
    (Manchester)
Marshall, Morgan & Scott
    (London)
McGraw–Hill (New York)

Edwin Mellen Press (Lewiston,
    NY)
Mercer (Cork)
Mercer University Press (Macon,
    GA)
Methuen (London *or* New York)
Humphrey Milford, Oxford
    University Press (London)
Milwaukee Public Museum
    (Milwaukee)
Gerd Mohn (Gütersloh)
J.C.B. Mohr (Tübingen)
J.C.B. Mohr [Paul Siebeck]
    (Tübingen)
Mohr Siebeck (Tübingen)
Mossad Harev Kook (Jerusalem)
Mouton (The Hague)
Mouton de Gruyter (Berlin)
Mowbrays (London)
John Murray (London)

Thomas Nelson (London)
Neukirchener Verlag
    (Neukirchen–Vluyn)
New Left Books (London)
Max Niemeyer (Halle *or*
    Tübingen)

Northwestern University Press
    (Evanston, IL)
W.W. Norton (New York)
Noord-hollandsche Uitgevers-
    Maatschappij (Amsterdam)

Oliphants (London)
Oliver & Boyd (Edinburgh)
Georg Olms (Hildesheim)
Orbis Books (Maryknoll, NY)
Oxford University Press (London
    or Oxford *or* New York)

Pantheon (New York)
Pardes Publishing House (New
    York)

Paternoster Press (Exeter *or* Carlisle)

Patmos (Düsseldorf)

Paulist Press (New York *or* Mahwah, NJ)

Penguin Books (Harmondsworth *or* London)

Pergamon Press (Oxford *or* New York)

Peeters (Leuven)

Pickering & Inglis (London *or* Basingstoke)

Pickwick Press (Pittsburgh)

Pittsburgh Theological Seminary (Pittsburgh)

Polebridge Press (Sonoma, CA)

Pontificio Istituto Biblico (Rome)

Pontifical Biblical Institute Press (Rome)

Praeger (New York *or* Westport, CT *or* London)

Prentice–Hall (Englewood Cliffs, NJ)

Presses Universitaires de France (Paris)

Princeton University Press (Princeton, NJ)

Putnam's Sons (London *or* New York)

Random House (New York)

Georg Reimer (Berlin)

Friedrich Reinhardt (Basel)

Fleming H. Revell (New York)

Rieder (Paris)

Rivingtons (London)

Routledge (London)

Routledge & Kegan Paul (London)

Royal Asiatic Society (London)

Royal Irish Academy (Dublin)

SBL (Missoula, MT *or* Philadelphia)

Schenkman (Cambridge, MA)

Schnell & Steiner (Munich)

Schocken Books (New York)

Schola Press (Austin, TX)

Scholars Press (Atlanta *or* Chico, CA *or* Missoula, MT)

School of Oriental and African Studies (London)

Schuman (New York)

SCM Press (London)

Charles Scribner's Sons (New York)

Seabury (New York)

Secker & Warburg (London)

Sheffield Academic Press (Sheffield)

Smith, Elder & Co. (London)

Soncino (Hindhead, Surrey *or* Jerusalem)

Southern Illinois University Press (Carbondale, IL)

SPCK (London)

St Benno (Leipzig)

Verlag St Gabriel (Mödling)

Stein & Day (New York)

Talmudical Research Institute (New York)

Tel Aviv University (Tel Aviv)

Temple University (Philadelphia)

Teubner (Leipzig *or* Stuttgart *or* Berlin)

Texas Christian University Press (Fort Worth)

Thames & Hudson (London)

Theologischer Verlag (Zürich)

Theologischer Verlag Rolf Brockhaus (Wuppertal)

Thornton Butterworth (London)

Tipograpfia Enrico Ariani (Florence)

Alfred Töpelmann (Giessen *or* Berlin)

Trinity Press International (Valley Forge, PA *or* Harrisburg, PA)

Trinity University Press (San Antonio, TX)

Trübner (Strasbourg)
Tyndale Press (London)

Undena Publications (Los Angeles)
United Bible Societies (London *or* New York *or* Stuttgart)
Universitätsverlag / Vandenhoeck & Ruprecht (Freiburg/Göttingen)
Université de Lille (Lille)
Universitetsforlaget (Oslo)
University Microfilms (Ann Arbor, MI)
University of Arizona Press (Tucson)
University of Birmingham Press (Birmingham)
University of California Press (Berkeley)
University of Chicago Press (Chicago)
University of Michigan Press (Ann Arbor)
University of Minnesota Press (Minneapolis)
University of New Mexico Press (Albuquerque)
University of North Carolina Press (Chapel Hill)
University of Notre Dame Press (Notre Dame)
University of Pittsburgh Press (Pittsburgh)
University of Texas Press (Austin)
University of Utah Press (Salt Lake City)

University of Wales Press (Cardiff)
University Press of America (Lanham, MD)

Vallentine, Mitchell & Co. (London)
Van Gorcum (Assen)
Vandenhoeck & Ruprecht (Göttingen)
Viking (New York)
Vintage Books (New York)

Waisenhaus (Halle *or* Braunschweig)
Wayne State University Press (Detroit)
Weidenfeld & Nicolson (London)
Weidmann (Berlin *or* Hildesheim)
Western North Carolina Press (Dillsboro, NC)
Westminster Press (Philadelphia)
Westminster / John Knox Press (Louisville, KY)
John Wiley & Sons (New York)
Williams & Norgate (London)
Carl Winter (Heidelberg)
Wissenschaftliche Buchgesellschaft (Darmstadt)
Word Books (Waco, TX, *or* Dallas)

Yale University Press (New Haven)

Zondervan (Grand Rapids)
Zwingli-Verlag (Zürich)

28. Sheffield Academic Press and JSOT Press

28.1 The name of the publisher of books that are now in the list of SAP has not always been Sheffield Academic Press. Until 1994 the name JSOT Press was also being used, and in 1989–1991 some books were published under the imprint Almond Press. This state of affairs is not a little confusing, and it is not surprising that authors frequently cite the publisher's name of Sheffield books incorrectly, especially for those titles that were published under the imprint JSOT Press when the copyright holder was Sheffield Academic Press. The following table sets out the details of the correct publisher's name (that is, the imprint, not the copyright holder's name) for all the books, by series.

BIBLE & LITERATURE SERIES
Almond Press

BIBLICAL SEMINAR
JSOT Press 1-14, 16-20, 22-23, 25
Sheffield Academic Press 15, 21, 24, 26 onward

COPENHAGEN INTERNATIONAL SEMINAR
Sheffield Academic Press

DICTIONARY OF CLASSICAL HEBREW
Sheffield Academic Press

FEMINIST COMPANION TO THE BIBLE
JSOT Press *Song of Songs*
Sheffield Academic Press all others

GOSPEL PERSPECTIVES
JSOT Press

GENDER, CULTURE, THEORY
Sheffield Academic Press

GUIDES TO THE APOCRYPHA AND PSEUDEPIGRAPHA
Sheffield Academic Press

HISTORIC TEXTS & INTERPRETERS
Almond Press

INTERVENTIONS
Sheffield Academic Press

JPT SUPPLEMENTS
Sheffield Academic Press

JSNT SUPPLEMENTS
JSOT Press 1-30, 32-98, 100-103
Almond Press 31
Sheffield Academic Press 99, 104 onward

JSOT/ASOR MONOGRAPHS
JSOT Press

JSOT MANUALS
JSOT Press 1-11
Sheffield Academic Press 2 (2nd edn), 12 onward
series title is Manuals from 12 onward

JSOT SUPPLEMENTS
Department of Biblical Studies, University of Sheffield 1, 5
JSOT 2-4, 6-10
JSOT Press 11-67, 72, 74-77, 79-81, 83, 86-87, 89-91, 93-96, 98-107, 110-111, 113-115, 117-169, 171-176
Almond Press 68–71, 73, 78, 82, 84, 85, 88, 92, 97, 108, 109, 112, 116
Sheffield Academic Press 148 (2nd edn), 170, 177 onward

JSP SUPPLEMENTS
JSOT Press 1-11, 13-15
Sheffield Academic Press 12, 16 onward

MANUALS *see* JSOT MANUALS

NEW TESTAMENT GUIDES
JSOT Press *John, Acts, Ephesians, Revelation*
Sheffield Academic Press all others

OLD TESTAMENT GUIDES
JSOT Press
except Sheffield Academic Press *Numbers, Joshua, Ruth and Esther, 1–2 Kings, Proverbs, Isaiah 1–39*

PLAYING THE TEXTS
  Sheffield Academic Press

READINGS
  JSOT Press *Qoheleth, Isaiah, Matthew, John*
  Sheffield Academic Press all others

SEMITIC TEXTS & STUDIES
  JSOT Press 1
  Sheffield Academic Press all others

SOCIAL WORLD OF BIBLICAL ANTIQUITY
  Almond Press

STUDIES IN SCRIPTURE IN EARLY JUDAISM & CHRISTIANITY
  JSOT Press 1-2
  Sheffield Academic Press 3 onward

29. Greek Characters

29.1 *The Names of Greek Letters.* Greek letters are referred to in English spelling, in roman type, when mentioned in the text. They are spelled thus: alpha, beta, gamma, delta, epsilon, zeta, eta, theta, iota, kappa, lambda, mu, nu, xi, omicron, pi, rho, sigma, tau, upsilon, phi, chi, psi, omega.

29.2 *Transliteration of Greek*

α	β	γ	δ	ε	ζ	η	θ	ι	κ	λ	μ	ν	ξ	ο	π	ρ	σ	ς	τ	υ	φ	χ	ψ	ω
a	b	g	d	e	z	ē	th	i	k	l	m	n	x	o	p	r	s	s	t	u	ph	ch	ps	ō

Rough breathing is indicated by an initial *h*.
Iota subscript is not indicated in transliteration.
γγ is transliterated *ng*, γκ by *nk*.

29.3 *Greek Fonts.* Sheffield Academic Press uses the SymbolGreek font, supplied by Linguist's Software Inc., Box 580, Edmonds, WA 98020-0580, USA. The keyboard layout in SymbolGreek is the same as in SSuperGreek and Graeca.

29.4 *Letters in English Order*

Lower Case

α	a	ι	i	ρ	r
β	b	κ	k	σ	s
χ	c	λ	l	τ	t
δ	d	μ	m	υ	u
ε	e	ν	n	ω	w
φ	f	ο	o	ξ	x
γ	g	π	p	ψ	y
η	h	θ	q	ζ	z
				ς	Shift `

Upper Case

A	A	I	I	P	R
B	B	K	K	Σ	S
X	C	Λ	L	T	T
Δ	D	M	M	Υ	U
E	E	N	N	Ω	W
Φ	F	O	O	Ξ	X
Γ	G	Π	P	Ψ	Y
H	H	Θ	Q	Z	Z

29.5 *Old Greek and Other Characters*

ϟ	Shift Option h	ϛ	Shift Option p
ϙ	Shift Option k	Ϝ	Shift Option z
ϻ	Shift Option m		

29.6 Punctuation

·	:	}	Sh Opt o	{	Opt o
(	(	[	Opt 9	;	Opt ;
)	)	]	Opt 0		

29.7 *Overwritten Accents, Breathings and Subscript*

᾿	j	῀	[	ᾶ	Shift
῾	J	῁	]		Opt /
´	v	῎	Shift \	῀	Opt /
`	;	῍	\	ᾶ	`
῾	{	῀	Opt 6	῀	>
῾	}				

29.8 *Accents and Breathings Not over a Letter*

᾿	Opt j	῀	Opt [	῀	Shift Opt i]
῾	Shift Opt j	῾	Opt]	῎	Opt \
´	V	῾	Shift Opt [	῍	Shift Opt \

29.9 *Emphasis in Greek Type.* Greek type is not italicized; if emphasis is required, the words are set in bold.

30. HEBREW CHARACTERS

30.1 *Names of Hebrew Letters.* Hebrew letters are referred to in English spelling, in roman type, when mentioned in the text, in these forms: aleph (*or* 'aleph), beth, gimel, daleth, he, waw, zayin, heth (*or* ḥeth), teth (*or* ṭeth), yod, kaph, lamedh, mem, nun, samekh, ayin (*or* 'ayin), pe, sade (*or* ṣade), qoph, resh, sin, shin, taw. SAP writes *kethib* and *qere*.

30.2 *Names of Hebrew Grammatical Forms.* Hebrew verb conjugations (voices, *binyanim*) are referred to in English spelling, in roman type, as: qal, piel, niphal, pual, hiphil, hophal, hithpael, polel, polal, etc. (abbreviated qal, ni., pi., pu., hi., ho., htp., pol., polal, etc.).

30.3 *Size of Hebrew Type.* Hebrew type that is in a paragraph of roman type should be larger than the roman type (14 pt in 12 point type, 16 pt in 14 pt type), e.g.

> In this 12-point sentence in English, the Hebrew verb
> קטל (14 point) is 'to kill'.

30.4 *Transliteration of Hebrew.* For certain purposes, such as naming Hebrew letters (§30.1) or citing the names of ancient Hebrew texts (e.g. §24.13-14) the exact, 'scientific' transliteration is not employed. Some SAP authors use a modern Hebrew system of transliteration (§30.7), and such is usually acceptable. Sometimes also a relatively well-known Hebrew word (e.g. *kabod, nephesh, ruach*), or one that is used repeatedly in a chapter or book, can be stripped of its scientific diacritics or otherwise be normalized in the direction of English. For the most part, however, words and phrases from the Hebrew Bible and ancient Hebrew texts, when transliterated, should conform to the system set out below.

30.5 *Consonants.* Hebrew consonants are transliterated according to the following system:

א	ב	ג	ד	ה	ו	ז	ח	ט	י	כ	ל
ʾ	b	g	d	h	w	z	ḥ	ṭ	y	k	l

מ	נ	ס	ע	פ	צ	ק	ר	שׂ	שׁ	ת
m	n	s	ʿ	p	ṣ	q	r	ś	š	t

Dagesh lene is not shown; dagesh forte is shown by doubling the letter.

30.6 *Vowels.* Hebrew vowels are transliterated according to the following system (accompanied in this table, for convenience, by the letter ב):

בַ	a (pataḥ)		בְ	e (šᵉwâ)
בָ	ā (qāmeṣ)		בִ	i (ḥireq)
בָה	â (final qāmeṣ hē)		בִי	î (ḥireq yōd)
בֲ	ᵃ (ḥāṭēp pataḥ)		בָ	o (qāmeṣ ḥāṭûp)
בֶ	e (sᵉgōl)		בֹ	ō (ḥōlem *defective*)
בֵ	ē (ṣērê)		בוֹ	ô (ḥōlem *plene*)
בֵי	ê (ṣērê yōd)		בֳ	ᵒ (ḥāṭēp qāmeṣ)
בֶי	ê (sᵉgōl yōd)		בֻ	u (qibbûṣ)
בֱ	ᵉ (ḥāṭēp sᵉgōl)		בוּ	û (šûreq)

30.7 *Modern Hebrew Transliteration.* Although it is the Press's policy to use the foregoing system of transliteration (§§30.4-6) for words and phrases from the Hebrew Bible and other ancient Jewish texts, some authors prefer to use one of the systems for the transliteration of Modern Hebrew. Such a choice is acceptable, though authors and editors alike should be careful not to mix the 'scientific' style and the more informal style.

א	ב	ג	ד	ה	ו	ז	ח	ט	י	כ	ל
	v	g	d	h	w	z	ch	t	y	k	l
										o r	
										kh	

מ	נ	ס	ע	פ	צ	ק	ר	שׁ	שׂ	ת
m	n	s		p	z	k	r	s	sh	t
					or					
					ts					

In this system, aleph and ayin are not transliterated, or else, before a vowel, transliterated with an apostrophe. The length of vowels is not indicated in this system, the vocal shewa is usually omitted, and doubled letters (dagesh forte) are ignored.

30.8 *Keyboarding of Hebrew.* All the Hebrew letters, vowels, accents and sigla in the critical apparatus of the the standard editions of the Hebrew Bible (e.g. *Biblia hebraica Stuttgartensia*) are available in the font Hebraica, which SAP uses. The font is available from Linguist's Software Inc., Box 580, Edmonds, WA 98020-0580, USA. Not all of the characters on that font are listed here—only those generally employed in books published by SAP.

30.9 *Consonants (Letters) in Hebrew Alphabetic Order*

א	ב	ג	ד	ה	ו	ז	ח	ט	י	כ	ך	ל	מ	ם
a	b	g	d	h	w	z	j	f	y	k	opt k	l	m	opt m

נ	ן	ס	ע	פ	ף	צ	ץ	ק	ר	שׁ	שׂ	שׁ	ת
n	opt N	s	[	p	opt p	x	opt x	q	r	c	c	opt c	t

For a dot in any of these letters, use the Shift form of the letter, e.g. b = ב, B = בּ.

30.10   *Hebrew Consonants (Letters) Grouped by Shape*

ו	w	ב	b
ז	z	כ	k
ן	n	פ	p
ג	g		
י	y		
		ד	d
ו	opt-N	ך	opt-k
ץ	opt-x	ף	opt-p
		ר	r

ה	h		ל	l
ח	j			
ת	t		מ	m
			ט	f
צ	x		ס	s
ע	[		ם	opt-m
א	a			
			ק	q
שׁ	c			
שׂ	v			
שׁ	opt-c			

30.11 *Vowels.* The vowels are usually centred beneath the letter; but some are above, and some are further to the right.

30.12 *Most Common Vowels*
This list shows the usual vowels beneath the letter בּ = b.

b]	בֵ		b}	בֵ
bi	בִ		b' (b, opt-])	בֶ
be	בֵ		b' (b, opt-})	בֶ
b;	בְ		bo	בֹ
b,	בֱ		b' (b straight quote)	בְ
bu	בֻ		bW	בוֹ

If 'Smart Quotes' have been turned on, they must be turned off in order to type the pataḥ (בַ); turn them off by typing the full stop (period) on the numeric keyboard (or, if you do not have a numeric keypad, by using your designated Command key(s) for Smart Quotes).

30.13 *Exceptions to Combination of Letter and Vowel.* With certain letters, different keystrokes must be used to position the vowels correctly.

30.14 *Narrow Letters.* With narrow letters, i.e.

ו	ז	נ	ג	י
w	z	n	g	y

use the Shift forms of the vowels, e.g.

zO	וֹ	z<	וֻ
zE	וֶ	zI	וִ
zU	וֻ	z option-[	וֳ
z:	וְ	z" (double straight quote)	וֹ

But the vowels with Option keys or Shift need not change.
Note: Do not use wO for וֹ; there is a special key: / (= וֹ).

30.15   *Unbalanced Letters.* With unbalanced letters, i.e.

ד	ר	ל
d	r	l

use the Shift form of the two vowels /;/ /,/ and the Option form
of the vowel /o/, thus, for example:

d Shift-;	דַ	r Shift-,	רָ
d Option-o	ד	l Option-o	לֹ

Option forms of the other vowels are used only when there are
other accents as well beneath a letter.

30.16   *Vowels inside a Letter*

דֻ	option-U	דֶ	option-E
דְ	option-:	דֳ	option-<
דֹ	option-"	דִ	option-K

30.17   *Other Notes on Vowels*
1. When the long *o* vowel and the shin-sign are both needed on a
shin, type v plus shift-O (i.e. שֹׁ).
2. After the letter qoph, a long *o* is to be typed with Option-o
(e.g. קֹסְמִים).

30.18   *Emphasis in Hebrew Type.* Hebrew type is not italicized
nor set in bold; if emphasis is required, the words are underlined.

31. Typesetting Parameters

31.1 At Sheffield Academic Press, the standard page size for printed books and journals is crown royal (before 1995, it was demy). Parameters used in Word 5 on the Macintosh for this size are (measurements are stated in inches):

paper size	US letter	
margins	top	1 in
	bottom	0.6 in
	left	1.403 in
	right	1.5 in
tabs	first	0.1875 in (3/16 in)
	others	add 0.1875
text	point size	14 pt
	line spacing	17 pt
margins for text	1/8 in from left	
footnote numbers in text	point size	9 pt
	superscript	5 pt
indented quotes, tables	point size	12 pt
	line spacing	15 pt
footnotes	point size	12 pt
	line spacing	15 pt
footnote numbers	point size	12 pt
	superscript	normal
	followed by tab	at 3/8 in
tabs in footnotes	right tab at 1/2 in	
	left tab at 5/8 in	

quotes, tables	point size	10 pt
in footnotes	line spacing	13 pt
table of	point size	12 pt
abbreviations	line spacing	15 pt
appendices,	point size	12 pt
excursuses	line spacing	15 pt
bibliography	point size	11 pt
	line spacing	14 pt

31.2 All text that is sent to the printer as camera-ready copy (see further §3.19 above) is set and printed on a laser printer by the Press according to these parameters, in order to create the sharpest image; it is then reduced by the printer in order to make the normal text size about 10 pt.

31.3 The Press uses various fonts for its books and journals, but especially New Century Schoolbook, Palatino and Times Roman. Times is chosen for a longer than average book, since it is most economical of space. For Greek text, the SymbolGreek font or Graeca is used (see §29); for Hebrew, the Hebraica font (see §30 above).

32. Differences between SAP and SBL Housestyles

32.1 The Society of Biblical Literature (SBL) has established a housestyle, which is published from time to time in its *Journal of Biblical Literature,* and also appears in Scholars Press's *Handbook for Editors,* pp. 37-59, as 'Instructions for Contributors'. This is the most complete set of housestyle rules for authors and editors of works in biblical studies apart from the present Manual, and many SAP authors will be familiar with it. Some of the significant differences between SAP style and SBL style have been noted elsewhere in this Manual at the appropriate point; in this section all the differences that have been noted are brought together systematically.

32.2 SAP accepts manuscripts in either British or American spelling, SBL only in American spelling.

32.3 SBL requires that italic type not be used. SAP requests that it not be used in manuscripts submitted in hard copy only (in which underlining is preferred), but prefers the use of italics to underlining when a disk version is being submitted.

32.4 SBL asks for special material (e.g. lists, tables, charts, diagrams) to be produced on sheets separate from the main text. SAP does not.

32.5 SBL requires a space to be left between the initials of persons (e.g. J. Q. Doe); SAP requires no space between initials, and only a space between the last initial and the surname (e.g. J.Q. Doe, J. Doe).

32.6 SBL prints quotations of five lines or more as indented paragraphs in smaller type; SAP prints quotations of four lines or more or of 40 words or more, and notes that the rule is not applied rigidly (see §18.3).

32.7 In references to biblical texts, SBL uses the form Gen 4:6. SAP prints Gen. 4.6, that is, with a full stop after the biblical book name if it is an abbreviation and not a contraction (see §17.2), and with a full stop and not a colon between the chapter and the verse.

32.8 In references to intertestamental literature and the Mishnah, SBL uses a colon (e.g. *Jub.* 14:4, 1QS 9:11, *m. Sanh.* 2:4). SAP uses a full stop in all such cases (e.g. *Jub.* 14.4, 1QS 9.11, *m. Sanh.* 2.4).

32.9 In references to works by ancient authors, SBL has no comma after the author's name (e.g. Homer *Il.* 24.200; Eusebius *Hist. eccl.* 3.3.2); SAP does (e.g. Homer, *Il.* 24.200; Eusebius, *Hist. eccl.* 3.3.2).

32.10 Footnotes are required by SBL to be gathered together at the end of the article or chapter; SAP asks for them to be printed at the foot of the page if possible.

32.11 Page and column numbers are not preceded by 'pp.', 'cols.' and the like in SBL style; they are so preceded in SAP style.

32.12 Publishers' names in SBL style do not contain 'Press', 'Verlag' and the like except in the case of a university press (but Scholars Press and Neukirchener Verlag [because Neukirchener is an adjective] are to be given in those forms). SAP uses the forms adopted by the publisher (e.g. SCM Press, E.J. Brill), except that it does not include 'Co.' or 'Ltd' or 'Inc.' and suchlike notations of the legal status of the publishing company (see §27.3).

32.13 In noting the series in which a book is published, SBL has no comma between the series name and the number; SAP does (e.g. VTS, 15).

32.14 In noting the series of a book, SBL writes, for example, SBT 2/5, meaning Studies in Biblical Theology, Second Series, number 5. SAP writes SBT 2.5.

32.15   Volume numbers of multi-volume works are indicated in SBL style with Arabic numerals (e.g. *TDNT* 6.44-55), but in SAP style with Roman numerals (e.g. *TDNT*, VI, pp. 44-55).

32.16   In the transliteration of Hebrew, SBL style uses special characters for aleph and ayin (ʾ and ʿ), SAP the closing and opening single quotation marks respectively (' for aleph, ' for ayin).

32.17   Abbreviations and acronyms are generally the same in SBL and SAP style. The following are the only observed differences (though note that, unlike SBL style, SAP style uses a full stop after an abbreviation of a biblical book name, though not after a contraction, that is, where the last letter of the contraction is the same as the last letter of the full word; thus Mt., Lk., but Mk, Jn):

SBL	SAP	
1–2 Chr	*1–2 Chron.*	*1–2 Chronicles*
Esth	*Est.*	*Esther*
1–2 Esdr.	*1–2 Esd.*	*1–2 Esdras*
Matt	*Mt.*	*Matthew*
Mark	*Mk*	*Mark*
Luke	*Lk.*	*Luke*
John	*Jn*	*John*
EpJer	*Ep. Jer.*	*Epistle of Jeremy*
Odes Sol.	*Odes*	*Odes of Solomon*
T. 12 Patr.	*T. XII Patr.*	*Testament of the Twelve Patriarchs*
Prot. Jas.	*Prot. Jas*	*Protevangelium of James*
Bib. Ant.	*LAB*	Pseudo-Philo, *Liber Antiquitatum Biblicarum*

33. Glossary of Publishing Terms

33.1 *Acid-Free Paper*
Paper designed to last at least one hundred years. All SAP books are printed on acid-free paper.

33.2 *Backlist*
Books that were published more than twelve months ago and that are still in print.

33.3 *Binding*
The process of folding, gathering, sewing and gluing the printed sheets of a book and of attaching the cover.

33.4 *Bleed*
To extend the printed image (usually a graphic) to the very edge of the page.

33.5 *Body (of a book)*
All the material of a book apart from the front matter and end matter.

33.6 *Book Face*
A font that is suitable for the text of a book, such as Times, Palatino, Bookman, Garamond.

33.7 *Camera-Ready Copy*
The text of a book printed on a laser printer and sent to the printer (book manufacturer) to be photographed onto film plates.

33.8 *Caps*
Capital letters.

33.9 *Cased*
Hardbound, hardbacked.

33.10 *Character*
A single letter or symbol. Word processors usually count the number of characters in a file. There are on average about 6 characters per word (counting the space between words), and about 2400 characters per average printed page.

33.11 *Colour Separation*
The process of preparing several different photographic images of the one graphic, which are to be overprinted in order to create a full-colour graphic.

33.12 *Copy-Editing*
The careful preparation of a typescript for typesetting.

33.13 *Copy-Editor*
At SAP, the copy-editor may be one of the Press's desk editors or a freelance copy-editor. The task of a copy-editor is to prepare a manuscript for typesetting and, usually, to read the proofs. See also *Desk Editor*. See §8.

33.14 *Copyright*
The legal protection afforded to books and journals. SAP normally assumes the copyright for books and journals it publishes. Authors are free to reprint articles or chapters of their own in other publications (with due acknowledgment). Requests from other persons to reprint an article or chapter by an SAP author are usually granted, but a fee is charged.

33.15 *Crop*
To trim an illustration (graphic) or to mark on an illustration the area that is to be reproduced.

33.16 *Depth*
The vertical measurement of type on a page.

33.17　*Desk Editor*
At SAP, the desk editors work full time at the Press's offices. Their duties are to supervise the passage of each title through the various stages from manuscript to finished book. Desk editors copy-edit a number of titles themselves, but they also manage several freelance copy-editors. Once a manuscript has been accepted for publication, the desk editor to whom it has been assigned is the Press's primary contact with the author, whether or not that desk editor is copy-editing the manuscript personally. See also *Copy-editor*. See §8.

33.18　*Display Type*
Type that is 18 points or more, or that is larger, bolder or distinctive. Display type is commonly used for advertising and for title pages, and rarely in scholarly books for headings and chapter titles.

33.19　*Ellipsis*
A character (...) that signifies the omission of one or more words.

33.20　*Em*
A unit of measurement equivalent to the width of the letter 'm'; thus an 'em-dash' is the character —.

33.21　*En*
A unit of measurement equivalent to the width of the letter 'n'; thus an 'en-dash' is the character –.

33.22　*Flush*
Aligned vertically. Thus a line that is set 'flush left' starts at the left-hand margin and is not indented.

33.23　*Font*
A set of characters and symbols that have been designed to harmonize with one another. See *Book Faces, Display Faces*.

33.24　*Front Matter*
All the material preceding the body of the book. Also known as

prelims. It includes half-title, series title page, title page, bibliographical page, dedication (which may be on the bibliographical page), table of contents, tables of plates, maps, illustrations, foreword, preface, acknowledgments, abbreviations, list of contributors—though not every book will contain all these elements.

33.25   *Gutter*
The space between columns on a page, or, the inside margin of a page.

33.26   *Half-Title*
The right-hand page preceding the title page, containing the title of the book and little more. Books in SAP series use the half-title page as the series title page. Not all books have a half-title page.

33.27   *Half-Tone*
The usual form of reproduction of a black-and-white photograph.

33.28   *Hanging Indent*
The format of a paragraph when the first line is flush left and the remaining lines are all indented.

33.29   *Hard Copy*
Typescript or laser-printed text, as distinct from disk copy (an electronic copy).

33.30   *Imprint*
The name of the publisher that is to be cited in bibliographic matter. The name of the publishing company is not necessarily that of its imprint, and one publishing company may have several imprints (e.g. JSOT Press and Almond Press were at one time imprints of Sheffield Academic Press).

33.31   *Inputting*
Typing a manuscript on a computer in a word-processing program. Also called keyboarding. At SAP, the manuscript has already been copy-edited when it is input.

33.32 *Justify*
To make a line of text, regardless of the length of the words in it, exactly the same length as others in the same paragraph or book.

33.33   *Leading*
The amount of space between lines of type. Typically, a line set in 12 point Palatino, for example, has a space of 14 points between the base of one line and the base of the next.

33.34   *Line Drawing*
An illustration without tones or shadings, e.g. a diagram or a drawing in pen and ink.

33.35   *List*
The list of all titles published by a particular publisher, whether in print or forthcoming.

33.36   *Monograph*
A specialized scholarly study, as distinct from a textbook (for classroom and student use) and a trade book (for bookshops and the general public).

33.37   *Manuscript*
While its etymological meaning is 'written by hand', the term is now used for the typescript submitted by an author to a publisher.

33.38   *OCR*
Optical Character Recognition, a method of reading typed or printed matter into electronic form.

33.39   *Orphan*
A short line ending a paragraph, at the top of a page. See also *Widow*.

33.40   *Page Extent*
The number of pages in a printed book, whether or not they are numbered. If there are blank pages at the end of a book, the page

extent is larger than the number of pages quoted in bibliographic entries.

33.41 *Perfect Binding*
A binding in which all the pages of the book are glued to one another and to the cover; while commonly used for paperback novels, it is not favoured as a binding method for books that are intended to have a long life.

33.42 *PostScript*
A page-description language for the computer which records not only the characters on the page but also their position, as well as the appearance and position of graphics. If a publisher sends a book to the printer on disk, it is in the PostScript language.

33.43 *Point*
A unit of measurement for type, equal to 1/72 of an inch. Books are usually printed in type of about 10 points.

33.44 *Prelims*
See *Front Matter*.

33.45 *Printer*
A desk-top machine for printing out one copy of a page; it is usually an ink-jet printer or a laser printer. 2. The firm that manufactures books and journals from the camera-ready copy, or disks, sent to them by their typesetters or by the publisher.

33.46 *Print Run*
The number of copies printed. SAP does not usually print more than 1000 or 1500 copies at the first printing. Occasionally more copies are printed than are bound; the sheets of the unbound copies are in such cases stored until sales justify binding them.

33.47 *Proof*
A printout of the electronic (disk) form of the book. SAP produces at least three proofs of a book in the course of the book's production.

33.48 *Royalties*
Sums paid to authors as a share of income from sales.

33.49 *Sans Serif*
Any typeface (font) without serifs, i.e. cross strokes at the top and base of characters. Geneva is the name of one such font. Sans serif is normally used for display lettering, not for the text of books.

33.50 *Serifs*
The cross-strokes, decorations and flourishes at the edges of characters. Typefaces with serifs are normally used for book work because of their readability.

33.51 *SGML*
Standardized General Markup Language is a set of notations for marking features of the contents and components of texts, e.g. different levels of headings. Embedded in the text of a document, SGML enables a single text to be output in a variety of formats.

33.52 *Sheets*
Sets of pages that have been printed but not bound. Sometimes only part of the print run of a book is bound at first, and sheets of the remainder are stored until they are needed.

33.53 *Signature*
Or, quire. A large sheet of paper containing many printed pages (usually 8, 16 or 32) of a book or journal. When a signature is folded and trimmed it forms a 'section' of the book.

33.54 *Smart Quotes*
Round quotation marks (' or "), in two forms, opening and closing. Distinct from 'straight quotes' (' or "), which do not look so well in printed text, and which do not indicate the opening and closing of the quoted matter.

33.55 *Spine*
The bound edge of a book, the part visible when books are shelved.

33.56 *Trim Size*
The size of the page, exclusive of the binding.

33.57 *Unjustified Text*
Or, ragged right. Text in which the right-hand margin is ragged.

33.58 *Widow*
A short line ending a paragraph at the foot of a page. See also *Orphan*.

34. CHECKLIST OF SPELLINGS, CAPITALIZATIONS, ABBREVIATIONS AND ITALICIZATIONS

34.1 Spellings peculiar to British style are flagged (UK); those peculiar to American style are flagged (US).

4 m thick wall
10 per cent increase
14-feet-thick wall
AAR (American Academy of Religion)
abridgment
accommodate
acknowledgment
ad loc. (in the appropriate place)
advertise
advise
aesthetic
aetiology
affect (cause, influence)
ageing (UK)
aging (US)
all right
allusion (reference)
am (before midday)
among (*not* amongst)
analyse (UK)
analyze (US)
ancient Near East
Arabic numerals
archaeology (UK, US)
BA (degree)
backlist
Bible
biblical
book of Psalms
bookshop
c. (*not* ca., *ca.*), *circa* (about)

cf.
christological(ly)
Christology
compromise
consensus
contra
cooperate
cooperative
copy-editor
cross-reference
cu. in.
data (is a plural noun)
dependant (noun)
dependent (adj.)
descendant
desk editor
disc (UK, but disk for computers)
discreet (having discretion)
discrete (separate)
disk (US)
Dr
dustjacket
e.g.
ecstasy
effect (execute)
embarrass
end matter
enfant terrible
enterprise
Epistles (a group of epistles, such as Paul's)
esp.

et al.
etc.
exercise
Fig.
focused
focuses
focusing
footnote
forbearance
forebear (ancestor)
foreword
forgo
freelance
front matter
frontlist
ft (foot, feet)
fulfillment (US)
fulfilment (UK)
full-fledged
fully fledged
Galilaean (UK)
Galilean (US)
Gentile
Gospel (one of the four
    Gospels)
gospel (the preached gospel)
Graeco-Roman (UK)
Greco-Roman (US)
handwritten
harass
Hasmonaean (UK)
Hasmonean (US)
Hellenistic
hereunder
high confidence-levels
high-quality workmanship
higher-level synthesis
holistic
Holy Spirit
housestyle
idem
i.e.
ibid. [to be avoided]
illusion (appearance)
improvise

in-house
in., ins. (inch, inches)
indiscernible
indispensable
infrastructure
infringement
insistence
inter alia
inter-regional
interdependence
interpretative (UK)
interpretive (US)
italic (type)
Jewish
Jewish-Christian author
    (hyphen)
Jewish–Christian tension (en-
    dash)
Jr
Judaean (UK)
Judean (US)
judgment
kg (kilogram)
King David
king of Israel, the
king, David the
lit.
lower case
lower-case letters
Lukan
m (metre)
m. (mile)
m^2 (square metre)
MA
Maccabaean (UK)
Maccabean (US)
Markan
markup
Matthaean (UK)
Matthean (US)
mediaeval (UK)
medieval (US)
Messiah (as equivalent to a
    proper name)
messiah (as a common noun)

messianic
microenvironment
millenarian
millennium
MLA (Modern Languages Association)
Mr
Muslim
n.p. (no place name given)
near-death experience
NEH (National Endowment for the Humanities)
nineteenth century
nineteenth-century development
no one
non-biblical
non-food-producing adults
non-gender-inclusive
nonexisting
nontextual
NS (New Series)
NW (north-west)
NY (New York state)
occurrence
one-sided view
one-year-old child
op. cit. [to be avoided]
OS (Old Series)
over-interpretation
over-long
pace
Pentateuch(al)
per se
Pharaoh, the pharaoh
PhD
Pl. (Plate)
pm (after midday)
postexilic
postmodern
pre-empt
pre-exilic
pre-existing
precede
preindustrial

primaeval (UK)
primeval (US)
principal (adj.)
principle (noun)
prise (extract)
program (US)
programme (UK, but program for computer program)
proofreader
psalm(s) (this psalm, these psalms)
Psalms (in reference to the book of Psalms)
q.v. (which see)
rabbinic
re-emphasized
re-evaluation
re-excavated
redaktionsgeschichtlich
rereading
resistance
Revd
Roman numerals
roman (type)
s.v. (*sub verbo*)
SBL (Society of Biblical Literature)
scriptural
Scripture
SE
Second Temple
Semitic
Septuagint(al)
sheikh
site-size data
Sitz im Leben
SNTS (Societas Novi Testamenti Studiorum)
sociopolitical
SOTS (Society for Old Testament Study)
Spirit (in reference to the Holy Spirit)
sq. in.
St (Saint, street)

stationary (adj.)

stationery (noun)

supervise

threefold

today

Torah (the five books of Moses)

traveled (US)

travelled (UK)

twofold

UK

up to date (postpositive, e.g. the book is up to date)

up-to-date (prepositive, e.g. an up-to-date book)

US, USA

vis-à-vis

while (*not* whilst)

wordprocessor

worldwide

worshiper (US)

worshipper (UK)

35. INDEXING PROCEDURES

35.1 The following rules enable the author or indexer who is working in Microsoft Word (on the Macintosh) to embed indexing tags in a manuscript before its pagination has been finalized. Then, once the final proof has been approved, the index(es) can be quickly and accurately generated automatically.

35.2 One advantage of embedding index tags within the text of the book itself is that when the book is to be issued in CD or some other electronic format no new indexing work needs to be done.

35.3 The procedures for embedding index entries in text are in principle straightforward; the complications that become apparent in what follows are due largely to the peculiarities of indexing biblical references, and in part from the need to cover all the eventualities.

35.4 Rules for the preparation and structure of indexes can be found in Section B of this Manual. What follows at this point is a sequence of procedures for indexing text in Microsoft Word.

35.5 *Keyboard Commands*
Certain keystrokes (shortcuts) should be set up in order to facilitate the process. They need to be set up only once for each machine. You can choose which keys will be assigned to the relevant commands, but a set that have been found to be convenient are the following:

> ⌘ (i.e. Command-semicolon) for Index Entry
> ⌘' (i.e. Command-apostrophe) for Hidden Text
> ⌘" (i.e. Command-shift-apostrophe) for Show Hidden Text

35.6 These keystrokes are assigned in the following way. Under Tools on the menu, choose Commands. When the list of Commands appears at the left of the dialogue box, scroll down to

Index Entry. Select Index Entry, and at the right of the dialogue box click on Add. A new dialogue box will open, asking for the keystroke you wish to enter. Type Command followed immediately by semicolon (⌘;). The keystroke will now appear in the box labelled Keys, and, once you have closed the dialogue box, it will be operational. The same instructions should be followed for setting up the keystrokes for Hidden Text and Show Hidden Text.

35.7 If you are making several indexes (e.g. authors cited, biblical references, subject index), it is a good idea to prefix the entries for the subject index, for example, with a character (like / or \) that will cause all the items for that index to sort together.

35.8 *Show Hidden Text*
To begin with, turn on Show Hidden Text (to which you have now probably assigned the keystrokes ⌘"). You should have Hidden Text showing throughout the whole indexing procedure. If you want from time to time to check that your index entries have not disturbed the text proper, you can type ⌘" to switch off Hidden Text, and type it again to switch it back on. The characters that are in Hidden Text will show with a row of small dots below; in these instructions, exceptionally, underlining is used to represent Hidden Text (otherwise the examples given here will not print out correctly and they will be indexed in the Index of the Manual itself!).

35.9 *Entering Index Entries for Authors' Names*
Work through the text, inserting index entries for authors' names, in this way: When you find an author's name, select it, and type ⌘;. For example, you find Smith. When you select it (by double-clicking) and type ⌘; you get <u>.i.</u>Smith<u>;</u> (that is, the Index Entry marker begins with <u>.i.</u> and ends with <u>;</u> both the prefix code and the end code being in Hidden Text). If the name is at the very end of a paragraph, there is no final <u>;</u> to end the entry; the paragraph marker serves to mark the end of the index entry. Smith is now flagged as an index entry for that page. Note that Hidden Text is shown on screen with a dotted underline (and in

these instructions with a normal underline), but on a printout the Hidden Text is invisible unless you have specified Print Hidden Text on the print menu.

35.10　You may choose to index only surnames. In that case, when you have run the indexing program, you will need to type in the initials of each quoted author from the Bibliography, distinguishing where necessary different authors with the same surname. Experience has shown, however, that it is less trouble in the long run to enter the full initials of each cited author at the point in the text where the name occurs. (Note that although the author's forename(s) may be given in full in the text or the footnote only the initials are required for the index.) Thus if the text mentions Smith, your indexed text should have, for example, .i.Smith, L.A.;, or, if the name is at the end of the paragraph, .i.Smith, L.A.

35.11　*Entering Index Entries for Biblical References*
When you find a biblical reference, the procedure is basically the same as for authors' names, but there are more points to take care of. If the form is Gen. 21.15, you select the whole reference, and type ⌘; and it will look like this—.i.Gen. 21.15;.

35.12　If the form is Gen. 21.15; Exod. 12.19, you do the same to each reference in turn, with the result looking like this: .i.Gen. 21.15;; .i.Exod. 12.19;.

35.13　If the form is Gen. 21.15; 32.19, you obviously need to repeat the Gen. for the second reference. The way to do this is: select 32.19, type ⌘; then Cursor Left and type Gen. plus space. The result will look like this: .i.Gen. 32.19;. That is, the second Gen. and its following space are in Hidden Text.

35.14　If the reference has a chapter or verse number less than 10, you need to insert a zero before the number, otherwise the index will not sort properly. So, for example, if the reference is Gen. 22.1, select the whole reference, type ⌘; to create the Index Entry, then Cursor Right to turn off the Select, then Cursor Left to position it in front of the 1, then ⌘' to turn on Hidden Text, then 0. The result will look like this: .i.Gen. 22.01;. It will print as Gen. 22.1 but it will index as Gen. 26.01.

35.15 If the reference is just a verse number, you need to supply in Hidden Text both the book and the chapter number. So, for example, if the reference is (v. 6) and you know that it is Gen. 12.6 that is being referred to, take these steps: Select the 6, type ⌘; to create the Index Entry, Cursor Left to turn off the Select, type ⌘' to start Hidden Text and type Gen. 12.0. The result will look like this: (v. .i.Gen. 12.06;).

35.16 *Indexing the Footnotes*
Footnotes cannot have Index Entries in them, so you need to copy or retype the words you want to be indexed into the text proper. Such entries should follow immediately after the relevant note number. The best way of proceeding is to split your screen with only two or three lines for the text and the rest of the window for the footnotes. When you have finished indexing one footnote, scroll the footnote window up until the next footnote number is at the very top of the footnote window; you will find that the corresponding footnote number in the text is on the top line of the text window.

35.17 When you find an author's name or biblical reference in the footnote, copy it and paste it immediately after the footnote number in the text. If there is more than one author's name and/or reference in the footnote, copy them all into the text at the same point, without any spaces between the names and/or references. Then Select one name at a time and make each into a Index Entry in Hidden Text, by typing both ⌘; *and* ⌘'. The result will look like this, with a footnote number followed by names and references in Hidden Text: thus, for example, 2.i.Smith, J.A.;.i.Jones, M.B.;.i.Brown, C.S.; and then the text continues.

35.18 *Making the Final Form of the Index*
These are the procedures for running the program that creates the index(es).

35.19 *Linking the Files*
If the work consists of more than one File, you need to link the

Files so that the Index is created for the whole work at one pass. Open the first File for the work, and go to Document under Format. Select File Series and type in the first page number of the first file. Click on Continue, and click on Next File. Open the next file in the series. Click on Reset Next File. Continue until all files have been linked. No page numbers need be inserted for the second and subsequent files. Refer to *Microsoft Word User's Guide (Version 5.0)*, p. 226, if in any doubt.

35.20   *Running the Index*
Open your first file, and click anywhere in it. Choose Index from under Insert. Usually choose Nested Format. When you type Return, MS Word will repaginate the entire set of files, and then run through the pages again, picking up the index entries. It will insert the Index at the end of the last file. If the Index is likely to be more than 1500 entries, use the Index Characters feature in the Index dialogue. Tell it, for example, to make an index for the characters A to M first, and then, when that has been completed, make a separate index for N to Z.

35.21   *Cleaning up the Index*
All index entries will have been sorted in one sequence, author's surnames, biblical references and subject entries (if any) alike. Separate the different indexes items into different files (your author's surnames entries may all begin with \ for example, and your subject entries with /, depending on how you have chosen to enter the data).

35.22   If you want page numbers to be preceded by a tab (as SAP does with biblical references indexes), follow this sequence: Replace all cases of comma, space (,) by comma, $ (,$), and all cases of full stop, space (.) by full stop, $ (.$). Replace all cases of space ( ) by Tab (^t). Then replace all cases of $ ($) by space ( ). You will then have changed

Gen. 12.06 2		Gen. 12.06	2
Gen. 21.15 1	into	Gen. 21.15	1
Gen. 22.01 2		Gen. 22.01	2
Gen. 32.19 1		Gen. 32.19	1

35.23 The next step is to remove unnecessary zeros by Replacing all cases of full stop, zero (.0) by full stop (.). The references will remain in their correct sorted order.

35.24 *Headings*
You should then type headings for each group of references, e.g. *Genesis* for the Gen. references, and delete all the examples of 'Gen.' preceding individual references (either by holding down Option as you drag down the column of Gen. or by Replacing all Gen. plus space by nothing). You can arrange the references in biblical book order as you go.

35.25 *Format of the Index*
The Index that is provided automatically will look like this:

/Brown, C.D. 26
/Jones, B. 33
/Smith, A.L. 42, 55
Exod. 12.19 37
Gen. 12.06 23
Gen. 21.15 8
Gen. 22.01 61
Gen. 32.19 44

When it has been cleaned up, it will look like this:

INDEX OF BIBLICAL REFERENCES

Genesis		32.19	44
12.6	23		
21.15	8	*Exodus*	
22.1	61	12.19	37

INDEX OF AUTHORS

Brown, C.D. 26	Smith, A.L. 42, 55
Jones, B. 33	

35.26 *Problems to Watch out for*
It is important to decide and keep to your standard abbreviations for indexing biblical book names. If you sometimes use 'Gen.' and sometimes 'Gn.' (or even 'Gen' and 'Gen.') your

index entries to Gen. 1.11, for example, will not sort together, and it will take a long time to consolidate the list.

35.27 Most important, it is very easy, when you are typing or copying authors' names from the footnotes into the text to forget to put them in Hidden Text. The name then appears as part of the text of the book, beside the footnote number. For this reason, it is important to do the indexing *before* the final proof-reading of the book. It is next to impossible to find any such errors without reading the entire text.

36. PROOFREADING MARKS AND SAMPLE PAGE

Marginal Mark	Meaning	Mark in Text
⟨	insert these words or letters into the text (note that the insert mark goes *after* the material to be inserted)	⟨
∧ ⟨	insert a letter space in the text	⟨
⨍	delete letter(s)	/ or ⊢⊣ through letters
⨍	delete word(s)	⊢⊣ through word(s)
⌢	close up letters/words, do not leave a space	⌢
⨍	delete and close up	⊤
⟨caps⟩	change to capitals	circle letters
⟨lc⟩	change to lower case	circle letters
⟨sc⟩	change to small capitals	circle letters
⟨rom⟩	change to roman	(wavy line under italic)
⟨ital⟩	change to italic	underline word(s)
⌣	transpose letters or words	⌣
∕ or ¦	separates two marginal marks on the same line	
⟨run on⟩	do not start a new line or paragraph	⌐
—⊏	leave a line space	
⟨close up⟩	remove a line space	( ) to left and right of the space
ʾ ʿ	insert apostrophe/opening quotation mark or closing quotation mark	⟨
ʾ ʿ	replace character by a closing or opening quotation mark	strike through character

The character's)personalities are revealed by their reactions

to the judgements. Both Saul and David accept the

condemnations made by Samuel and Nathan and confess their

sins. Saul says, 'I have sinned; for I have transgressed the

commandment of the Lord and your words' (1 Sam. 15:24), and

David says, 'I have sinned against the Lord.' This

self condemnation reveals *both* the negative and the positive

aspect of the character.

37. Typesetter's Alterations ('Disk Cleanup')

37.1 When a manuscript is received on disk, the Press's type-setters regularly carry out a number of procedures in order to conform the author's manuscript more closely to the Press's housestyle. These changes are not marked on any proof the author will receive, since they are in many cases both numerous and minor. But since it is the Press's policy that authors should be aware of all changes introduced into their manuscripts, the following list of provided of the changes that fall into the category of preliminary alterations ('disk cleanup').

insert even and odd headers

replace two spaces by one (there is no circumstance in which two successive spaces are allowed to stand)

convert straight quotation marks to 'smart quotes' (rounded quotation marks)

change space-hyphen-space to em-dash

change three dots to the ellipsis character

convert caps to small caps when necessary (e.g. BCE)

change format of biblical references to housestyle when necessary (including abbreviations of the names of biblical books)

change order of closing quotation marks and fullstop, etc. as necessary, in accordance with §§15.7-8

38. For Further Reference

Butcher, Judith, *Copy-Editing* (Cambridge: Cambridge University Press, 1972, 1981)

Fowler, H.W., *A Dictionary of Modern English Usage* (Oxford: Oxford University Press, 2nd edn, 1983)

Gibaldi, Joseph, *MLA Handbook for Writers of Research Papers* (New York: The Modern Language Association of America, 4th edn, 1985).

[Gilmer, Harry W.], *Handbook for Editors* (Scholars Press Handbook Series, 5; Atlanta: Scholars Press, 1992)

Hanks, Patrick (ed.), *Collins Dictionary of the English Language* (London: Collins, 1979)

Hewitt, R.A., *Style for Print and Proof-Correcting* (London: Blandford Press, 1957)

Judd, Karen, *Copyediting: A Practical Guide* (Menlo Park, CA: Crisp Publications, 2nd edn, 1990).

Macintosh, E. (reviser), *The Concise Oxford Dictionary of Current English* (Oxford: Clarendon Press, 1951)

The Chicago Manual of Style (Chicago: University of Chicago Press, 13th edn, 1982)

INDEX

a, and *an* 57
abbreviations 48, 72-76, 106, 122-
    27, 128, 142
  avoided in headings 54
  avoided in running heads 55
  checklist of 174-77
  in small caps 75
  list of common 75
  of ancient Jewish works 103,
    109
  of Dead Sea Scrolls 111
  of Early Christian literature
    109
  of Hebrew terms 75
  of Josephus's works 103, 111
  of metric measures 72
  of Midrash Rabbah 102
  of Midrashim 102
  of Mishnah tractates 101
  of Nag Hammadi tractates 126
  of periodicals 128-42
  of Philo's works 103, 110
  of Pseudepigrapha 108
  of rabbinic texts 124
  of reference works 128-42
  of serials 128-42
  of Talmud tractates 101
  of Tosefta tractates 102
  of US state names 87
  SAP vs. SBL style 165
  size of table of 162
  vs. contractions 72
  when not to be used 128
  without full stops 75
  words never abbreviated 75
acid-free paper 21
  defined 166
acknowledgments 48
acronyms 128
  SAP vs. SBL style 165
  without full stops 72

address list 10
address of SAP 10
an, and *a* 57
ancient Jewish works
  abbreviations of 103, 109
ancient texts
  form of names in indexes 100
  indexes of 98
  references to
    without Roman numerals
      60
  SAP vs. SBL style 164
Apocrypha
  canonical order of books 106
  position in indexes 100
  SAP vs. SBL style 164
apostrophe
  insert (proofreading mark)
    185
appendix 49
  size of 162
Arabic numerals
  for chapter numbers 53
  for level 3 headings 54
  for numbers of journal issues
    60
  in chapter numbers 74
  in heading numbers 53
articles
  capitalization of 71
author
  compound names 98
  disagreement over housestyle
    51, 59
  form of name 83, 84
  initials of
    SAP vs. SBL style 163
  list of works by the same 48
  name
    in bibliography 83
    in chapter title 53